YOU ARE
A
BADASS
MOM

A Guide to Take your Life, Love, and Parenting to the Next Level

STEFFANI LEFEVOUR

STEFFANI LEFEVOUR

ISBN: 978-1-9863-2121-1

YOU ARE A BADASS MOM

This book is dedicated to the man who finally "broke my ass" and made me a mom. Thank you for always believing in me, babe…even with something so hard and so precious. And for loving me the way my soul needs loved. You have given me more than I ever dreamed was possible. I always knew you'd make a great Dad. I was right.

And to the woman who taught me what life is all about. Who showed me how to maneuver through it with strength and perseverance. Who was always there for everything. From Girl Scouts, and heartbreak. To band gigs and triathlons. Your notes and cards and advice never go by unnoticed. Thanks mom. I couldn't do this parenting thing without you.

And of course to the two little schnootenbootz who chose me as their mom. And who taught me more about life and love than I ever thought possible. For every swear word, homework fight and middle of the night snuggle I am grateful. You are the light and the way. I will always follow you. And will love you no matter what.

CONTENTS

FOREWORD   7

INTRO TO AWAKENING   11

AWAKENING 1: AWARENESS   25

    PERSONALITIES   26

    LOVE LANGUAGES   34

    BADASS HOMEWORK   37

    FOURTEEN LIFE CATEGORIES   39

    BADASS HOMEWORK   45

    RADICAL ACCEPTANCE   46

    UNIVERSAL ASSIGNMENTS   51

    BADASS HOMEWORK   54

    UNDERNEATH THE SURFACE   54

    BADASS HOMEWORK   61

    S+S+S=R   62

AWAKENING 2: YOUR STATE   66

    GRATITUDE   67
    BADASS HOMEWORK   71
    MORNING ROUTINE   72
    BADASS HOMEWORK   78
    OVERWHELM   81
    BADASS HOMEWORK   86
    OUTSOURCING   88
    BADASS HOMEWORK   91
    GET THESE OFF YOUR PLATE: 93
    THE POWER OF LETTING GO   95

AWAKENING 3: YOUR STORY   98

    AUTOMATIC NEGATIVE THOUGHTS   99
    SUBCONSCIOUS THOUGHTS   105
    CANCEL PROCESS   110
    BADASS HOMEWORK   112
    AFFIRMATIONS   113
    BADASS HOMEWORK   116
    LIMITING BELIEF WORK   118
    THE POWER OF INTENTION   121
    FOCUS ON THE GOOD   124
    HAPPINESS   129
    BADASS HOMEWORK   133
    FUTURE PULLS   139
    BADASS HOMEWORK   142

AWAKENING 4: YOUR VISION 144

BOUNDARIES 145

BADASS HOMEWORK 147

SURROUND YOURSELF WITH GREAT PEOPLE 149

BADASS HOMEWORK 152

UPPER LIMIT PROBLEMS 153

PLAN YOUR NEXT ADVENTURE 156

ACCOUNTABILITY 158

SAY YES 159

THE CLIMB 162

NEXT LEVEL 167

READING & RESOURCES MENTIONED 171

GRATITUDE 172

ABOUT STEFFANI 177

FOREWORD

DEAR MOM,

May I be frank?

I know you want to be a fantastic, amazing mom.

I know you want your children to be strong and resilient and brave. I know you want your sons and daughters to lead a life of love and compassion while having the courage to shine their light and live their truth. And let's be honest, I know you (secretly) want your children to think you're the most awesome mom now and forever.

Every mom wants to be a better mom, but few are willing to look in the mirror, tell the truth, and do what it takes to BE the mom they yearn to be.

That takes courage. And effort. And a willingness to be brutally honest with yourself.

That's the real sacred work of being a mother: excavating your soul to be the person worthy of your children. To be the role model they deserve.

To that end, your job is to face yourself ruthlessly with love and have the courage to do the hard work of shifting your behaviors and beliefs. When you do that, you will know how to be the calm in any storm and have the ability to accept "what is" in any downtrodden moment while being the soft place of love when the tears fall or the vase breaks.

And you're going to need a big ass toolbox to do it.

YOU ARE A BADASS MOM

Learning how to be a Badass Mom is the path that only the most fearless choose.

Steffani LeFevour has that kind of courage and is that kind of mom, and now, she generously shares her journey and her toolbox with you.

Through her gut-wrenching story, you will feel there is hope regardless of what kind of mom you've been in the past, and her tools will be the stepping-stones you need to be the Badass Mom you always prayed you could be.

Rhonda Britten, Master Coach
Named "America's Favorite Life Coach"
Founder of the Fearless Living Institute
Author, *Fearless Living* and Emmy® Award-
    winner

STEFFANI LEFEVOUR

INTRO TO AWAKENING

FIVE YEARS AGO, I had one of the lowest points of my life. Things didn't look bad on the surface. I had my own coaching business helping busy moms find more lasting happiness. I was living in my dream home. I was in good shape, working out four to five times a week. Eating healthy. My relationship was in a "good" place (always a work in progress after almost twenty years together). I should've been really happy. I was really happy.

But I was hiding a terrible secret. I was yelling at my kids. I was yelling at my kids *a lot*.

STEFFANI LEFEVOUR

My patience was nowhere to be found. Under the surface, I felt overwhelmed on a daily basis. Totally stressed. I was trying to juggle running my business with the logistics of raising two young kids and running a household. Let's face it, being the primary parent takes a lot of work. Being a working primary parent is like having two jobs. Make that three jobs, because you're also pulling the night shift.

I was completely depleted but had no idea that my life was in such bad shape until it all came crashing down around me. It was a typical Thursday night: My husband was at work, pulling his third shift of three straight fourteen-hour days (#workaholic), which is typical. It was a long day. A typical long day with two young kids.

And my kids are not easy kids. (Are any kids easy?) They're explosive, they can be aggressive, they fight a *lot*. It was hard for me, at the time, to be alone with them. I dreaded it, actually. (Insert feeling like a terrible mom for even writing that.)

So by Thursday night, I was ready for a break. I put them in the bath, put my game face on, and added some bubbles, trying to be the Instagram Awesome Mom. I was trying the best I could not to make too many demands, not to bark too many orders, not to be that awful controlling mom that I always feared I would be and yet...

When it was time to get out of the bath, I asked them politely to get out of the tub. They ignored me. I asked again. They complained. I asked again, they started fighting. I asked again, they whined and complained some more. I asked them *again*—they screamed and yelled, they splashed each other, they splashed me, and finally by my tenth or eleventh request— who knows?—I *exploded*. I screamed "*Get your asses out of the f***ing tub!*"

It got ugly. I turned into a complete monster. I grabbed a tiny three-year-old by the arm and yanked her out of the tub, her soaking wet body dragging across the floor, and threw her into her room. I went back for my son, grabbed him out of the tub, spanked him on his wet butt and threw him into his room. I'm sure I yelled and swore some more as they both sobbed, crying naked and wet on the floors in their rooms with no towels on and no loving mom to help them. The sight of bubbles trailing down the hallway was a terrible reminder of my dramatic, disgusting behavior.

Then I lost my shit. I melted on the floor in the bathroom while trying to sop up the water and bubbles all over the tile and I cried that awful guttural ugly cry.

Who am I? What kind of monster does something like this?

I was completely defeated. *Why isn't this*

parenting thing easier? What the hell is wrong with me? Who does that to their kids? They should put me in jail. Someone should call DCFS.

I heard my son's wet feet run down the hallway from his room to my daughter's room. More wailing and crying ensued. A minute passed, and I heard her door open. I was still on the bathroom floor, sobbing, sitting in suds and tears. Jack came out of the room and came close enough to the bathroom to yell, "Please don't hurt us."

"Please don't hurt us"? You can imagine my horror. My kids were now afraid of me. I'd turned into the monster mom that I see in reality TV shows. I was even worse than those moms.

I'm a flippin' happiness coach. I help people shift their mindset and find more happiness. What the hell was wrong with me?

That was the wake-up call that set off a

rocket of desire for me to do the work I needed to do on myself—to improve my parenting in a dramatic way and start showing up as the mom I knew my kids needed me to be. As the mom they deserve to see on a daily basis. Not just on Sundays at a family party, not just on social media, but even on a Thursday night after a long, hard day on her own. A mom that can hold her shit together even if dad's not around. Even with no wine. Even with the fighting and whining and splashing.

That mom seemed out of reach to me at the time. But I had a deep purpose to find her. I knew she was in there. She was deep in there, doing one-arm push-ups in the corner. My higher-self mom was always there, available to help me—I just wasn't letting her in. I didn't have the tools to know how to access her on a daily basis. On a Thursday-night-bathtub-scene basis.

YOU ARE A BADASS MOM

That night, I decided to improve my parenting, to find the patience that I needed to be the mom that I knew I could be. To take all the strategies that I used to take my business piece of my life to the next level and apply them to the parenting piece, the patience piece, the loving partner and wife piece. Although I felt like I was succeeding in a lot of areas of life, those more important, more meaningful areas were not where I wanted them to be.

I walked into my daughter's room and got real with my kids. I took 100% responsibility for what happened. I apologized for everything. I explained that it wasn't about the fighting or the whining or the splashing. It was about my fears. I was living in overwhelm. I was so afraid that I was terrible at this mom thing that everything they did "wrong" triggered me. Every little thing triggered an explosion.

I knew then that I needed to work on me. No parenting book was going to help. This wasn't about bedtime routines or positive discipline— this was about my shit. Me shifting my shit. I needed to start showing up as a better mom. I needed to live as my higher self, badass mom more often.

When I went to bed that night, I had another sign. For the previous six months, I'd had an evening routine where I wrote down three things I was grateful for, three things that were awesome about my day and one thing that could've made the day better. That night, I started flipping through the past six months of my notes and I saw a common theme: "I should've been more patient with the kids." "I shouldn't have raised my voice." "I shouldn't have snapped at Zoe." "I shouldn't have yelled so much." "I should've been more loving." "I should have been more present." "I should have put down my phone." There was massive shame and a lot of regrets, and they were all based on my patience, my kindness, my self-acceptance—and me not showing up as who I wanted to be.

I'm sure that, as a mom, you can relate to my shame. To the real raw truth of how hard this parenting thing can be at times. We all have our "bathtub" moments.

What followed after that dreaded Thursday night that we now refer to as "Mom's Mommy Monster Freakout" was a series of incredible events that led me to the biggest breakthrough of my life yet...

After reading my evening journal and dissolving into more tears, I got on my knees beside my bed. Literally. I know we see things like that in movies and don't do them often in real life, but this was an event that called for a grand gesture. I folded my hands on my bed and prayed for some help. I launched a rocket of desire to the Universe and said, "I release this situation to you. I know you can help.

Show me the way." I essentially "let go and let God." "Jesus take the wheel," as Carrie Underwood would say. And things started shifting almost immediately.

Two days later, I got a call from an Oprah producer. I was pretty surprised, but this didn't come out of left field—I had worked with Oprah before on a few things. This producer asked me directly if I had any challenges or struggles in my parenting. *What? Seriously? OK, Universe, let's do this.* "Yes, yes, Mr. Oprah Producer, I have plenty of struggles in my parenting." He then asked if I would be willing to participate in a Lifeclass with Oprah and Dr. Shefali Tsabary, the author of the amazing book *The Conscious Parent*.

Now when you ask the Universe to help you improve your parenting and an Oprah producer calls about that exact subject, you just say *yes*. You don't think about national TV or sharing your Mommy Monster Freakout story or how exposed you might feel sharing your deepest shame and biggest fears. You just say "yes."

That "yes" led to my big breakthrough. And here's the gist of it.

When I was young, I never thought I wanted to have kids. I feared I would be terrible at it. I thought it would be too hard. (Um, I was right about that.) I thought I would f*** up my kids and they would be awful kids because I was an awful mom. So every time they fought, splashed, exploded, it reiterated my biggest fear. They were awful because I was awful. They misbehaved because I was really bad at this mom thing. They exploded because I had no idea what I was doing.

After the Lifeclass, which I now call my intervention with Oprah, when the dust was settling, my husband sitting beside me totally mortified, looking like a deer in headlights (actually looking like a deer that had just been hit by a car), I had a profound and ugly breakthrough: I was essentially creating my biggest fear. My deepest, darkest fear, that I would be a terrible mom, was running my life. That limiting belief had taken over and I had no control over it.

Until now.

See, when you expose a deep fear, it no longer has control over you. When you pull a limiting belief up by the root, you can get rid of it forever. I changed a few things immediately. And surprisingly none of them involved drinking more wine (although that was my first thought).

First, I stopped bathing them every night. Duh, why didn't I do that sooner? It was a trigger for me, so I got rid of it. If they wanted to get clean, they could take a shower or bath but I was not going to go there for a while.

YOU ARE A BADASS MOM

Next, I forgave myself. I literally did a mini-ritual and said goodbye to "Mommy Monster" forever. It wasn't easy. It took a lot of strength, inner work, and conviction, but it's been years now since we've seen her so I finally feel like I have put Mommy Monster in a locked closet in the basement.

What also followed was the creation of four awakenings that helped me get up off that bathroom floor and back to my higher self. The four awakenings that took me from Mommy Monster to Mommy Master. (Well, maybe not quite "Master" yet, but at least "Mommy Who Doesn't Freak Out So Much.") These lessons have been developed from almost thirty years of personal development work. They've been adapted from the work of Marianne Williamson, Neale Donald Walsh, Deepak Chopra, Louise Hay, Thich Nhat Hanh, Pema Chodron, Brené Brown, Byron Katie, and Oprah (wow, a *lot* of Oprah). I applied these four awakenings to my parenting, to my life and to my relationship and my life is now unrecognizable from the way it was. Don't get me wrong—it wasn't bad back then. But it wasn't the highest version of myself that I knew I could be. The highest version of the life I knew, deep down, I deserved.

I share these awakenings in the hopes that it will help you take your life, love, and parenting to the next level. Or at least to help you avoid a Mommy Monster moment.

AWAKENING 1:

Awareness

AWARENESS IS THE MASTER discipline. If I didn't have that dark night of the soul on the bathroom floor that made me aware of that monster mom inside of me, I could never have turned it around. Awareness is the key to making powerful, positive change. There are a lot of things we need to bring into our awareness on a daily basis if we want to live our highest mom selves. If we want to be a Badass Mom and not a Monster Mom.

Personalities

The first thing I do with all my clients is help them understand the nature of their individual, unique personalities. I use a profound wisdom called the enneagram, an ancient personality test. Some say it dates back 4,000 years. It's the only personality test that I found that helps everyone clearly understand the unhealthy traits of their specific personality, the average traits, and the healthy traits. By understanding these, one can focus on being their best self, on constantly striving to live more in their healthy traits than their unhealthy traits. This line of mystical mathematics was passed on through Plato, Philo, and in Sufi traditions.

I found the enneagram work about fifteen years ago, and I've used it with hundreds of people since then. I used it in my previous career, when I was a director at a health club with hundreds of employees, and use it with every one of my clients now. Everyone I work with has to have an enneagram reading first, or we won't get everything we can out of our time together. That's how important this work is. It completely changed my life when I learned my enneagram number and really got to know more about myself and my personality.

Before knowing my enneagram number, I thought I was broken. Why were some things so easy for other people and so hard for me? Why wasn't everyone excited to travel the world and always up for a spontaneous adventure? The beauty in understanding your personality type is two-fold: First, there's comfort in knowing that you're not alone, and then there's another level of grace that comes from truly embracing that not everyone is like you.

I'm a seven, The Adventurer. When I first learned about my number, I finally understood why I always overloaded my plate with so many things. As a mom, it's great to know that sevens have an unhealthy habit of trying to do too many things at once. We want to do it all, see it all, stay up late, party until the sun comes up. Not easy to do when you have a baby at home.

Sevens also have "shiny object syndrome," so it's hard for us to specialize in one thing. This is why I never had fewer than three jobs at once, and why working a full-time job felt like a death sentence. It's also why when I went to Europe in my early twenties, I traveled to a different country every day. I jumped from Germany, to France, to Spain, to Portugal, like they were all about to disappear and I had to see them all at once. It's my nature. I'm afraid I won't get to it all so I must do it all *now*.

It's also hard for sevens to "settle down." Feeling domesticated is a huge trigger for me, and understanding my number helped me to get that. Sevens need a lot of variety. Not easy to find in a monogamous twenty-plus-year relationship. But it's possible. It's possible when you're a healthy seven, but not an unhealthy seven.

The enneagram is the only personality test that clearly defines a vision for you of the highest version of who you can become. Sevens, at their best, are visionaries. They are the most positive, happy and hopeful of all the numbers. (Great for a happiness coach and mindset mentor.) And their love of life can feel palpable to everyone around them. But only if they're healthy. Otherwise, they can look like a hot mess (just like every unhealthy number).

After I really absorbed everything about my number, I quickly found out my husband's enneagram number. And oh, wow, was that a game changer. Knowing his number and the details about who he was at his core helped me radically accept him for who he was, instead of thinking he needed to change and be more like me, or that he was broken and needed fixing. I focused on the healthy traits of his number and made a conscious effort to support him to live the highest version of himself. My husband is an eight, The Challenger. I used to think his Irish Catholic temper was his issue, but it was when I fully understood the enneagram work that I really got him. Challengers love to fight. Literally. They feel connection when there's a level of conflict in the room. They're afraid that the world is a dangerous place, so they protect everyone and themselves. They're also incredibly driven—thus, usually workaholics, and their drive to control their surroundings often leads them to many levels of success. Challengers at their best are extremely generous. They protect people. They help people up off their knees and give people many opportunities. When I understood all of this and stopped trying to change my husband from an eight into a seven, things dramatically improved in our relationship.

YOU ARE A BADASS MOM

There's a beautiful level of radical acceptance that comes from really knowing and understanding your personality type. Challengers don't love to travel, because they feel anxiety when they're not in control. Eights don't like to travel and sevens thrive on new experiences. Funny joke, Universe. But oh, the beauty that comes from the awareness and understanding of this. Now we're no longer striving to change each other—we just have radical acceptance for who we are, and support each other along the journey.

Imagine what it would be like to understand your kids' enneagram numbers. My kids are ages six and nine right now and I think I know what their enneagram numbers are. My daughter is most likely a six, The Loyalist. The same number as my best friend, Jen. Loyalists are loyal friends and family members, but they're also loyal to their opinions. They can be stubborn and come off as selfish when they don't have the space they need. They love to be at home alone, and need time for solitude. The first thing my daughter wants when I pick her up from school is to go home. She's a homebody. So different from me. Meanwhile, my son is a social butterfly, he might be a seven. He would never go home if he didn't have to. I totally get that. It's even hard for us to go to sleep at the end of the day. We never want to day to end. What if we miss out on something? #fomo

Understanding that our kids are unique and have their own individual personalities is powerful. Honoring what they need takes things to a different level. We often want our kids to be like us and do what we would do. Big mistake. When we aren't aware of our numbers or our personality traits and how different they most likely are from our kids, we're setting ourselves up to fail. Awareness is the key. (You'll hear me say that *a lot*.) Here is a graphic with a brief description of each type.

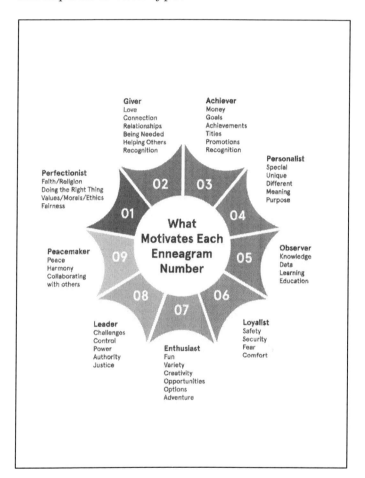

Don't assume you know your personality

type just from these titles. Email me and I'll send you some links that includes a deeper dive into the enneagram and helps you learn what number you truly are. You might be surprised at the results—you'll definitely be enlightened.

info@myhappilife.com

Love languages

I'm sure you've read or heard about the book *The 5 Love Languages* by Gary Chapman. Having an awareness of your love language, and those of your partner and kids, is key. My husband and I first met when he was only eleven years old and I was fifteen. (Yes. Holy shit. That long ago.) We started dating ten years later. We have an epic love story—notice I said *epic*, not easy. Where do you think those explosive kids come from? From explosive parents. We were together for more than ten years before I knew his love language or even knew my own.

YOU ARE A BADASS MOM

Awareness of your love language, understanding your love language and your partner's love language, can be life changing. See, we tend to give the love language that we want to receive. Until we get clear on the love language that we need and the love language that our partner needs, we can't deliver that. Never have I had a client whose partner had the same love language as theirs. It just doesn't happen. Another funny joke played by the Universe. My primary love language is quality time while my secondary love language is acts of service, and those are my husband two least important love languages.

My husband's primary love language is words of affirmation while his secondary love language is physical touch, and those are the least most important to me. It's not automatic for me to tell him how much I love him or how I appreciate him or how proud I am of all he has become. I don't need to hear that, and it's not how I feel loved, so it takes effort for me to give it. It isn't natural to me. We didn't do that in the house I grew up in—we still don't. Rarely do we say "I love you" in my family. But in John's family we say it all the time. Awareness is the key. (There it is again.) How I feel loved is when he shows up. Works out with me, comes to events with me, sits on the porch with me, just shows up to be near me. And that's hard for him to do because that doesn't make him feel loved. The awareness of and understanding our love language is crucial in a relationship.

It's important in our parenting as well—when we can understand our kids' primary love language, we can deliver that. Until we get clear on that, we're most likely just delivering the love language that we needed to receive as a child, and thinking that our own children should feel loved that way. A mom whose primary love language is acts of service might always make her kids' lunches and pick up their things and organize their homework, but unless that's their primary love language, that's not going to make them feel loved. Imagine if their love language is quality time and you're giving them gifts. Or their love language is physical touch and you're always giving them words of affirmation and leaving little notes in their lunch box. It's powerful to find out what makes our kids feel loved.

BADASS HOMEWORK

Here's a fun process that we did together as a family. We took the five love languages and wrote them out on five different pieces of paper.

We drew pictures for my daughter since she couldn't read yet.

1. Words of affirmation
2. Acts of service
3. Receiving gifts
4. Quality time

5. Physical touch

Each person took those five slips of paper and organized them from most important to least important. My most important was quality time. My husband's most important was words of affirmation. My son's most important was physical touch. And my daughter's most important was receiving gifts. It was interesting to learn that my eight-year-old son, who wasn't as cuddly and lovey and wouldn't let us kiss all over him like we used to, said his number one love language was still physical touch. What a beautiful thing to know. And no wonder my daughter begged and pleaded for "lovies" (what we call stuffed animals) every time we went anywhere. Because buying her things made her feel loved. Now I get it. Awareness is key.

Here's a graphic to help you understand your love language and learn the love languages of your family.

WHICH **LOVE** LANGUAGE?	HOW TO COMMUNICATE	ACTIONS TO TAKE	THINGS TO AVOID
WORDS OF AFFIRMATION	Compliments Affirmations Kind Words	Send notes or cards.	Criticism
ACTS OF SERVICE	Action words like "I Can", "I will", "What else can I do?"	Helping with house and yard chores. Repair/Maintenance. Acts of kindness.	Ignoring partner's requests while helping others.
RECEIVING GIFTS	Positive, fact-oriented information.	Give gifts on special occasions and also on not so special occasions.	Forgetting special days.
QUALITY TIME	One-on-one time. Not interrupting. Face-to-face conversation	Take long walks together. Do things together. Take trips.	Long periods of being apart. More time with friends than with partner
PHYSICAL TOUCH	A lot of non-verbal. Verbal needs to be "word pictures".	Touches Hugs Pats Kisses	Physical neglect or abuse.

Fourteen Life Categories

We also need to be aware of the fourteen different categories that that make up our lives. I learned these fourteen categories from an amazing, life changing program called *Lifebook* that I attended, then facilitated for many years and still work closely with, and I adapted them to fit my mom life. Information on this transformational personal growth experience can be found at www.mylifebook.com.

The fourteen different categories are:

Your Personal Life

1. Your Health and Fitness (number one for a reason)

2. Your Intellectual Life (this is also where your thoughts live)

3. Your Emotional Life (where your happiness lives)

4. Your Spiritual Life (and/or religion, and connection)

5. Your Character (all your values and traits)

6. Who You Show Up As in the World (kind of important)

Your Relationships

7. Your Love Relationship

8. Your Parenting

9. Your Extended Family

10. Your Social Life

Your Business Life

11. Your Career

12. Your Financial Life

Present and Future

13. Your Quality of Life

14. Your Life Vision

###

The first six categories make up the foundation of our lives. If that isn't solid, you can't build on it. Period.

If you don't have your health and fitness where you want it to be, your thoughts where you want them to be, your emotional life and your happiness really where you want them to be, your spiritual life and connection where they need to be, your character traits aligned with who you want to be, and you're not showing up in the world as who you really want to be, then you're building on top of shaky ground. You have a weak foundation.

Until you put energy attention and focus on those first six categories, only then can you build the relationships you desire. Only then can you be the parent you want to be. Only then can you create the bigger, better career and financial freedom that you really desire. All of that will lead to the next-level life that you're building. We need to work on us first. And as busy, driven ambitious moms, we normally put everything else first.

We're building a strong foundation here. We can't enhance our love relationship when our health and fitness and our emotional life are not where we want them to be. We can't be a great parent when our thoughts are spiraling out of control and we've given our love relationship zero attention. All of these categories are interconnected. But the six pillars of our personal life are the *solid* foundation that we need to build a life we love.

Here's a graphic to show you how these fourteen Life Categories all build on top of each other.

14 Categories of Your Life

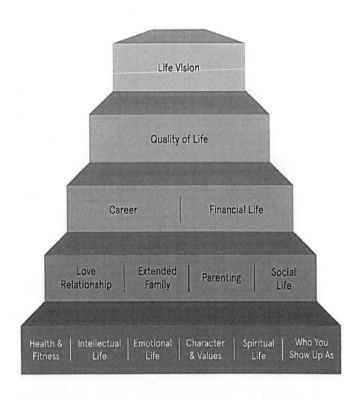

BADASS HOMEWORK

Here's an exercise you can do to find out where you rate yourself in every area of your life.

Get out your journal and write down each of the categories. Then give yourself a number between 1 (the lowest) and 10 (the highest) in each category, right next to each one. Be very honest with yourself. Think about what it would look like to have a 10 in each category. Are you there yet? Now, on a new sheet, start with the category that you have the lowest score in and write down what would it take to get to a 10. What would it look like if that category was a 10? Focus on how you would *feel*, and who you would be. Look at the categories you rated the lowest. Now you know where to start. Putting energy, attention, and focus on those categories that need the most work will help you create your next-level life. And remember: You are a badass mom. It's *totally* possible to get a high score in *all areas*. This is not reserved for a rare few—it's available to us all.

Radical Acceptance

When we have awareness of the six pillars in our personal life, and we're putting energy attention and focus on *ourselves*, on what we need to be the most badass mom we can be, then we can move on to our love relationship.

I believe every love relationship is a choice. There's not "the one" who's out there for each of us. There are a lot of options and we *choose* to make someone "the one."

I had the pleasure of hearing the amazing author and journalist Dan Savage speak at a conference and he shared his theory that there are a lot of .85s and .72s and .90s out there. We choose one of them and we round up and make that .85 or .92 our *one*. I love that theory.

YOU ARE A BADASS MOM

The power is in the choice. Once we *choose* that relationship then we need to *accept* that person, love them unconditionally. When we awaken to this *choice,* as opposed to a mistake or default or settling (all of which my clients have expressed—and be honest, our thoughts have all been there), then we can truly accept this *choice.*

Yes, we can still ask in a loving way for what we need. We can still hold each other to our greatest selves. We can still grow together. Grow individually. And enhance and improve our lives together. We don't need to stay stagnant. We can't stay stagnant. We're badass moms. And that means we're driven for more.

I often feel we focus more on how we need our partner to change then we do on our own growth and expansion. I'm guilty of this too. When I look at my husband and think about what HE needs to change...

He needs to be more positive.

He needs to pay more attention to me.

He needs to be more present.

Can I turn all of that around and see how I need to do the same? YES YES YES.

We buckled ourselves in to this roller coaster ride together. The ups and downs, the steep climbs, the free falls. All of it. Why would I ever complain about the ride? Or the price of admission?

If this is the price it's going to cost me to be with him, to go on this beautiful ride, to have this amazing life, then I am happy with it. I can accept it, love it, and even be grateful for it.

When I had this revelation after hearing Dan Savage, I immediately wanted to share it with John. Instead, I applied it first. What's the "price of admission" that I pay to be with him? A temper. Some negativity. Him working long hours. Not being present. Lack of communication. The fact that he never cleans up after making his late night PB&J. His Sunday naps that are timed perfectly with the kids meltdowns.

If that's the price of admission I have to pay for this life, to be with him and have these amazing kids and go on this roller coaster ride, then I'm all in. Hell, yeah.

This was a huge shift. This concept completely altered our relationship. Before, all I thought about was how those things needed to change. Now that I accept it as the price of admission, there's a different energy in the room and in our relationship.

And believe me, he pays a price to be with me. The fact that I love to travel. My obsession with personal development. My very detailed morning routine that involves, music, breath work and meditation. The supplements and superfoods that take over every cabinet in our kitchen.

Price of admission.

Is it worth it?

I sure hope so.

So I applied this lesson first before sharing it with John. And started looking at him very differently. I was more patient with him. I stopped trying to change him. I stopped chasing him around the kitchen, asking him to clean up his PB&J. And after about a month, I shared this lesson with him. I explained how it was helping me to be more unconditionally loving and accepting of him. He got it. And saw what my price of admission was.

Our love is a choice. Applying this price of admission concept can totally change your relationship and help you take it to the next level.

Universal Assignments

Also aligned with radical acceptance is accepting our Universal assignments. We're going deeper now and talking about why we're here. What's our meaning and purpose on this planet? What did we sign up for before we came here?

Do you know your Universal assignments?

I had a Universal assignment to lose my sister when I was eleven years old. I believe I signed up for that so that I would learn about loss very early on. And would be able to support others through loss later in my life.

I had a Universal assignment to have an alcoholic father. I chose him so that I would be independent and learn not to wait around for a man to save me. So that I would take 100% responsibility for my life and design it the way I want.

STEFFANI LEFEVOUR

I had a Universal assignment that school didn't come easy for me. And I placed an order for two kids that share the same struggle.

I also believe this is a reward life for me. That I am meant to prosper. Another Universal assignment. (Oh a positive one, how refreshing.)

My husband and I have a Universal assignment to be together and raise these kids together. And it's a Universal assignment that he has a temper and that we're so incredibly opposite. (Hint: these Universal assignments are also insights into the price of admission, mentioned earlier, meaning things we should not bitch about...)

My son being born early and with preemie issues was a Universal assignment. I was meant to experience that so that I would really understand what women go through, learn my own strength, and relate to women who have a hard time after having a baby.

YOU ARE A BADASS MOM

I have a Universal assignment to travel the world. It lights my soul on fire.

I have a Universal assignment to be surrounded by transformational leaders and amazing humanitarians so I'll be challenged to raise the bar and always inspired to do better.

I have a Universal assignment to teach what I know. I can't experience anything without then teaching it. It's ingrained in my DNA.

I have a Universal assignment to help moms find more lasting happiness and take their lives to the next level. It's why I'm here. It's what fulfills me.

What are your Universal assignments? Can you look at the challenges in your life as Universal assignments and radically accept them as that?

BADASS HOMEWORK

Take out your journal and write down your unique Universal assignments. The good, the bad and the ugly. What big overriding lessons and themes have you seen in your life? Bonus points if you can uncover why you chose them.

What hidden blessings did they bring into your life? Double extra bonus points if you can get into a place of gratitude for each and every one of them.If you're ready to be vulnerable and dare greatly, share your Universal assignments with your husband or mother or friend. Ask them about theirs. There are treasures in there waiting for you.

Underneath the Surface

Now, there's a lot more to be aware of. Our personality traits, our love language, the fourteen categories that make up our lives— those are things that are tangible, that we can measure. They're just the tip of the iceberg.

Then there's everything else below the surface. Those things that are harder to measure and define, like our thoughts. We create our thoughts. Our thoughts create our intentions. Our intentions create our reality. Are your thoughts important? Yes! Is every thought critical? Yes! Our thoughts are the light switch to our feelings. And sometimes we let them just ride on autopilot, thinking we don't control them. But now is the time for us to take over and fly the plane. (Teaser alert: Details on how to change our thoughts revealed in Awakening 3.)

In addition to our thoughts, we need to be aware of our stories. Those old self-sabotaging stories and limiting beliefs that we carry around with us like baggage. The self doubt and fear that no longer serve us. You know the one about how we're not enough. The one that tells us we're unlovable when we're real raw and vulnerable. The one that says that we can't earn as much money as a man can. The thought that we're not strong enough or smart enough or that we can't have it all. Yeah, those ones. The big and the small baggage that's holding us back from a life we truly love.

We need to be aware of the negative self talk that runs rampant in our mind and turns us into a Mommy Monster. I know you have those too. The negative self talk when you step on the scale and even if you're in good shape for you, you're still not happy with the number on the scale. Or you don't like your hair even the moment you step out of the salon. (Or is that just me?) This negative self talk can be considered abusive. If you talked to your child the way you talk to yourself in your head, you'd be ashamed. Let's bring some awareness to it so we can stop doing it for good.

We need to also be aware of our excuses.

YOU ARE A BADASS MOM

Our excuses are the accumulation of our thoughts and words combined to destroy our potential. Think of excuses as the anchors that are holding you back. The anchors you drop to stop your boat from flowing downstream.

We need to be aware of our triggers—those things that flip the Mommy Monster switch. Those things that try our patience and that turn even a beautiful Sunday into a shit show. Now here's the thing about our triggers: It's not the world's job not to trigger us. It's our job not to be triggered. When we uncover our triggers, we can change them. They're like these under-the-surface land mines, and we think everyone in the world (especially our kids and our husband) should know where they are and walk around them. Instead of expecting everyone else to avoid our triggers, we need to dig around under the surface to uncover them and get rid of them for good.

When my son was a baby, I realized that I

had a colossal trigger around being domestic. It was hard enough for me to take time off work and spend so much time alone. Add to that all the new tasks at hand: the washing and cleaning and pumping and bottle sanitizing. It was too much for this momma.

When my husband walked in the door one night and asked "What's for dinner?" Oh. My. God. Talk about a land mine. I had a reaction that I can't express in words. I wanted to jump out of the window and never return. It was my first glimpse of a *huge* trigger. Thank God, I was reading some Eckhart Tolle at the time and his explanation of our pain bodies resonated with me. Triggers, pain bodies—same thing. Those things that upset us and create a big reaction. My pain body was alive and well and she wanted revenge. (Breathe, Steffani, breathe) That's the power of our triggers.

Now, not only do I know what triggers me,

but I know what to do about it. I understand that it's no one else's job not to trigger me. I mean I can tell my husband about my domestication triggers (read that as *warn him*) and hopefully he will help and try not to step on that land mine but again, it's not his job. It's my job to remove it. To turn it from a trigger into a non-issue. What if the words he said when he walked in were different words? What if every time he said "What's for dinner," I interpreted that as "Wow, you're amazing"— that's my prerogative. We absolutely can turn our triggers into something positive. Because we are in control. No one else.

I had another issue that I turned into a positive. My phone was going on the fritz. It would freeze on me. In the middle of a text. While trying to post in my Facebook group. While answering an email to a client. It would just freeze. At the most inopportune times.

I noticed myself starting to get frustrated.

Picture me poking at my phone furiously over and over again, thinking it's going to start working any second. It would last a few seconds or many minutes. Totally unpredictable.

Once I was aware of it, I could shift it. I chose to use it as a Universal sign to slow down and be present. I would close my eyes and breathe and think of something I was grateful for. What a beautiful gift. Now it wasn't a frustrating trigger anymore, it was a welcome pause in my day. I savored them. And awareness is what got me there.

So let's bathe in awareness for a while. Let's look deeply under the surface and figure out who we really want to be. What does our healthiest, happiest self look like? Who do we really need to be to take our lives to the next level? And what limits, excuses, triggers, or negative talk is holding us back? This awareness alone can take help us take our lives to a place we once never thought it could be. A bigger, better more loving life awaits at the end of awareness.

BADASS HOMEWORK

It's time to look under the surface. Take out your journal, or who are we kidding, any piece of paper that you can find in the craft drawer, and journal on the following.

What are my top 3 triggers?

What are my top 3 excuses?

What are my top 3 limiting beliefs?

What are my top 3 fears?

What is really holding me back?

What can I do to take my life to the next level?

S+S+S=R

The last thing we need to be aware of is the three Ss that make up our reality. Here's a little formula I use:

Your STATE + Your STORY + Your STRATEGY = Your REALITY

When we want to change something in our life, we normally try and change our strategy first. Then that doesn't work and we try a new strategy. Then that doesn't work and we order another parenting book and we change the routine and we buy some new gadget and we make a new recipe and we hire a new personal trainer. Then we give up and pour another glass of wine. See, were going at it all wrong. Focusing on doing doing doing. On strategy strategy strategy. We focus on the action but we need to start with our state. If we're in the wrong state, and if our story isn't aligned with what we want, no strategy is going to work.

YOU ARE A BADASS MOM

Let me give you an example. Before John and I got married, I was trying to lose weight. I wanted to lose five to ten pounds before our wedding day. I started a new workout regimen, and I tried the latest diet trend, which I think was the Atkins diet at the time (not sure—I've tried them all). I was tracking my calories and burning 2500+ calories a day and only eating around 1500. I did a VO2 max test, had a personal trainer and a dietician.

Remarkably, I was *gaining* weight. It was mind-boggling. I was actually gaining fat. I know because I was testing it all the time.

When I look back on it now, I get it. I was stressed. Overwhelmed. And running on empty all the time. I drank only beer or wine, very little water. I worked out too hard and had too few calories, most likely. But here's the real killer: I was telling everyone and anyone who would listen that I was burning muscle and gaining fat. That was my story and I was sticking to it.

And it became my reality. My thoughts and words were that strong. They were defying science. When it finally hit me that I was adamantly placing an order from the Universe for what I didn't want. I changed things up.

First, I focused on my *state*, on how I felt every day, and then I created a new story, a new mantra.

My new *story* turned into "I'm burning fat and building muscle." "My body responds to everything good." I would sing it in the shower. And dance around my apartment joyously.

Once again, I let go and let God. I asked the big U to take over. I eased up on my workouts, started eating more food and guess what? With a new state and a new story, every *strategy* I tried was working.

YOU ARE A BADASS MOM

I was suddenly a fat-burning machine. I had a very high metabolism and, believe me, I told everyone who would listen about it.

Suddenly, even strategies that didn't work before started working. But it all started with my state *first*.

AWAKENING 2:

Your State

OUR STATE IS ALL about how we feel. How we prime ourselves to prepare for our day. The state that you're in every day will determine how you handle the challenges that are thrown your way, and we know that as badass moms, we will be handed a lot of challenges. Will we handle them with grace and ease or with struggle and frustration? Our state determines if we get triggered then spiral out of control and have a Mommy Monster moment or if we breathe and move through it peacefully. So what can we do every day to maintain our emotional intelligence? To handle those triggers and keep our state in check? Here are some ideas.

Gratitude

Do you have a gratitude practice? Going B.I.G. (Beginning In Gratitude) every morning can be the biggest and best state shifter. And it's not just good to have gratitude for breakfast—gratitude can help you shift at any time of day. See, you can't be frustrated and grateful at the same time.

If I had used this tool when my kids were splashing in the tub on that dreaded Thursday night and just sat my butt down on the radiator and thought about what I was grateful for, the Mommy Monster Freakout would most likely not have happened.

Gratitude is your best friend. If there's one tool that's *the* most important thing you can apply to your life (Okay, maybe second to awareness), it's gratitude. And usually we think we're grateful. We say we're grateful. We talk about having a gratitude practice. But we don't actually *do* it. How much do we actually apply gratitude to our life?

Here are some practices to try:

Gratitude jar: This sat on our kitchen table for more than a year. For an entire summer, we wrote down something we were grateful for every night around dinner and put it in the jar. When anyone was having a bad day, we reached into the jar to try and find some of our gratitude love notes. It always helped us shift.

Gratitude chalkboard: Every November, we have a big chalkboard in our kitchen, and we each write something on it every day that we're grateful for.

Gratitude sun salutations: I mentioned that I need variety. I've tried a ton of different gratitude practices. This one I keep coming back to. On a day when I'm not working out, I stand in a sunny spot in my family room, and I do twenty sun salutations, thinking of one thing I'm grateful for each salutation. Twenty is a lot. I even cover my siblings, our neighbors, my kids' teachers. It's awesome and a great workout.

The Five-Minute Journal: This is a book and an app. I love it. It should be called the one-minute journal. It takes thirty seconds every morning and thirty seconds at night to answer a few questions. Beautiful process.

Shower gratitude: When are we really grateful for our bodies? Every so often, I turn my shower into a gratitude shower. Thanking every inch of my body, every body part, every cell, for its health and vitality. Have you thanked your liver for functioning lately? Or your teeth for being strong? I doubt it. Try it—it's fun.

Good night gratitude: Every night (Okay, not *every* night—it goes in waves, but I try to do it every night), I ask my kids what went well that day and what one thing they're grateful for. That's a totally different bedtime routine then my Mommy Monster Freakout, eh? It always leads to some beautiful discussions. Focused on gratitude. Yes, please.

Thank you notes: In 2000, when I turned thirty, I ran the Chicago Marathon. That day, I wrote a thank you note to someone I ran into at mile twenty who helped me run those last 6.2 miles strong. And I decided to write one every Sunday for the rest of the year. That was in October, so I committed to do it for just two months. But I didn't stop then. I wrote one or more thank you note to someone in my life every Sunday for three years. I wrote to businesses, to friends, to family members, to my future self, to my guides and angels, to strangers, to my employees, to my mechanic, to my therapist, and to Oprah.

One year, I wrote 186 thank you notes. Not emails, not text messages (this was before texting), just a handwritten card. At the time, it was the most powerful thing I had ever done for my life. I was living in a perpetual state of gratitude. All week, I was thinking about who I would write to and what I was grateful for. What a powerful experience. I only stopped because I need variety and people were getting annoyed with my constant gratitude. You've been warned.

Nothing new can come into your life unless you're grateful for what you already have. Think about that for a second. Your life will expand and improve in direct proportion to how grateful you are for it and all that you have.

BADASS HOMEWORK

Now are you ready for an upgraded life? Then upgrade your gratitude practice. Commit to one gratitude practice that you will add to your life *starting tomorrow.*

If you're ready to be vulnerable and dare greatly, join me in my free Facebook group and share your new commitment. You'll find other moms who are committing to the same one and you'll inspire someone else along the way. This is *not* your average mom group. In our Badass Mom Society, we share our wins, we celebrate every small victory—we get real, raw, vulnerable, AND we focus on the good. We come together to support each other in living our highest selves. As they say "it takes a village." This is your village.

https://www.facebook.com/groups/badassmomsociety/

Morning Routine

Another big thing we can do for our state is to look at our morning routine. How you start your day makes a huge difference in how your day is going to unfold. The way you prime yourself every morning gets you prepared for the challenges that might be—that *will* be—thrown your way.

So what does your typical morning routine look like? Do you wake up and check Facebook? Do you answer emails right away? Is your day proactive and designed by you, or is it reactive to everything around you? What the kids need. What your husband needs. What your job needs. We're usually making all those demands a priority and not prioritizing what we need. When we consciously create our morning, we are back in charge of our state.

Here's what my old morning routine used to look like:

> ➢ Wake up with the kids running in my room complaining about having to go to school.
>
> ➢ Grab my phone and check Facebook to see if I got any likes or shares or

comment on my most recent posts.

➤ Stumble out of bed and help the kids get dressed.

➤ Bicker with my husband about who's going to make them lunch.

➤ Get them off to school while answering emails, barely looking at any of them while also thinking about having to squeeze in a workout before my first client.

As you can see, that morning routine would get me in a pretty frantic and overwhelmed state for the rest of the day. Thus, Mommy Monster Freakouts after dinnertime. It was completely unplanned and reactive.

My new morning routine, that's forever evolving, looks a little more like this:

➤ I wake up before the kids and go B.I.G., begin in gratitude. I close my eyes and think of at least five things that I'm grateful for about my life, five things that I'm grateful for about the work I do, and five things I'm grateful for about me, about who I am.

➢ I listen to a morning song to set the tone for my day.

➢ I then do the Five-Minute Journal, which consists of writing down three things you're grateful for, three things you'll do today to make the day great, and one "I AM" affirmation.

➢ When my kids come in, we play snuggle tickle fest.

➢ I drink a morning tonic, a healthy concoction that's not tasty but totally worth it.

➢ I have some one-on-one time with each of my kids.

➢ Instead of bickering with my husband, I try and connect with him in a special way before he leaves.

➢ When the kids go off to school, the first thing I do is sit down and meditate/visualize/do some breath work. I have a whole delicious process I go through to step into my big vision and really embody who I want to be and how I want my day to unfold.

➢ Then I head out the door for a workout. That also helps my state.

➢ I come home and make a green drink. That helps my state, too, and sets me up for a day of healthy eating. (Can you already see a massive difference in my day?)

➢ Then, before I do anything else, I track my habits in a daily habit tracker.

Before I tracked my habits, I was inconsistent. When I track my habits, I do them. It's that simple.

I have an accountability group who holds me accountable for everything. I've had accountability groups for different things in my life for more than twenty years. Accountability is key to creating new habits and actually doing them consistently.

By this time, it's only 10:00 am. I feel amazing and invincible. I'm ready to do some writing and hit the ground running, and I haven't checked Facebook or answered emails yet.

My entire morning is proactive, not reactive. Because it's so intentionally proactive, I can be ready for things that were unplanned, like seeing the kids' lunches on the kitchen counter after they've left for school. Or a neighbor knocking on the door for a favor. And I won't be thrown into a panic. Can you see how much more primed I would be to handle problems that might come up?

A morning routine sets up our day for success. That's for certain. But we need to find some things during the day that maintain our state as well. When we come home after school or after work to the kids, is there anything we can do to prepare for that? Maybe a little breath work in the car before we walk in the door or a little meditation? When we come in the house, can we light some candles or put on some fun music? Can we put down our phones and be present? What things can we do throughout the day to get us in the right state? To maintain this good vibe we have going? Our state is important. We should treat it that way.

BADASS HOMEWORK

Here's a little exercise you can do right now to change your state starting tomorrow.

If you're a visual learner (like me) I have a fun, free video to walk you through this process where we can go even deeper. And a worksheet.

YOU ARE A BADASS MOM

Because yay. Free worksheet.

www.badassmorningroutine.com

If you're not a free worksheet fan, take out a journal and start writing what your current morning routine is and be very real. List everything that happens on a typical morning for you.

Then write out your ideal morning routine. And I mean the big dream. Don't take any of your actual circumstances into account. Just dream big. Do you want to wake up and go for a walk on the beach? Do you want to have someone prepare a delicious breakfast for you? Just go for an ideal morning routine. There's a reason for this. When we dream flippin' huge, we open a portal for bigger, better things to come to us. I promise you can never dream too big. So go for it.

Now look at the difference between the two routines.

Now we're going to create an "ideal for now" morning routine. An "ideal for now" morning routine is so important because we're not always going to be in the ideal but it's good to have something to strive for and an "ideal for now" morning routine is what you can start doing tomorrow morning. Even if you're not in your dream home yet, what's ideal for now? Even if your kitchen is under construction what's ideal for now? Even if you're traveling a lot for work, what's ideal for now? When we can create an "ideal for now" morning routine we are in charge of our state again. We take our state back and we take our day back. When we can have a good day, that can lead to good weeks that can lead to good months and that can lead to an amazing badass year. Our state is that important.

Now for a challenge. Because you're a badass mom, I know you're ready for a challenge.

What can you commit to doing tomorrow to get yourself in a better state for your day?

Commit to it now. Grab your phone (I'll wait) and text your best badass mom friend and tell her what you're committing to. Or better yet, head over to our Badass Mom Society Facebook group and tell your new tribe.

https://www.facebook.com/groups/badassmomsociety/

One thing we love to do in there is drink wine together. The other thing we love to do is hold each other accountable for new habits that get our state in order. So join us. Let's get after this together.

Overwhelm

So here's where we talk about the big O word: not Oprah, (unfortunately), not orgasm (even more unfortunate), but Overwhelm.

This big O plagues *all* moms. Too many women fall prey to this monster. But as badass moms, it's got nothing on us. Or at least it won't any longer, once we take some action and make a few shifts.

Overwhelm comes from being *reactive* to your life. Reacting to everyone's demands on you. As badass moms who actually want to get shit done in this life, we need to become more proactive, less reactive. We need to take our days and our power back.

Here's my strategies for overwhelm. First, as usual, it starts with our thoughts. The more we *think* about overwhelm, the more we *talk* about overwhelm, the more we *feel* overwhelmed. Our thoughts are the light switch to our emotions. When we think it, we'll feel it. So we need to do the internal work around our thoughts, then also take action and physically change those things that are weighing us down and putting too much on our plates.

YOU ARE A BADASS MOM

Thoughts first. Always. What most moms tend to do is think about how overwhelmed they are. Many times a day. Literally fifty times a day would be an understatement, especially around the holidays or when someone is ill or when there's a lot of change going on, like back to school or moving your home. Think about it: If we think about being overwhelmed fifty-plus times a day, we have just placed fifty-plus orders to the Universe for more overwhelm. Add to that the thoughts that go with it, like:

* "I have no support."
* "My husband never helps out."
* "My kids are totally out of control."
* "No one picks up after themselves."
* "I don't have enough hours in the day."
* "There's no way I'll get everything done."
* "I have too much on my plate."
* "No one appreciates me."
* "This book will never get finished." (Maybe that's just me.)

* "This isn't fair."
* "I need more help."
* "Oh, really, you want a puppy? You have *got* to be kidding me!"

Fifty-plus times a day, we have the conscious and subconscious thought "I'm overwhelmed," then add all of the above in to the mix. How can we expect to be living in anything but overwhelm? We're drowning in overwhelm and that's exactly what we've asked for.

Okay, now we need to shift it. We have to change the thought of overwhelm and focus on the time we do have. We have to focus on the help and support we do get. We have to cancel the thought of overwhelm and replace it with a more powerful positive thought. Gratitude is a great shift. What am I grateful for? Phew. It can immediately diffuse overwhelm. (More processes on how to change your thoughts in the next chapter. Yep, we got this.)

The next key to combatting overwhelm is getting things out of your head and onto paper. The overwhelm comes from too much thinking. All the things we need to do that are not organized and not actionable are just all floating around in our heads.

"Oh shoot, that's right, I still have to email my daughter's soccer coach."

"Oh yeah, and I never got a baby shower gift for my niece."

"Wouldn't it be nice if I had a present for Jack's teacher on the last day of school?"

"Damn, I forgot to book a babysitter for Saturday night."

Those thoughts: I could list 1,000 more of them and not even scratch the surface of what a busy mom faces in a day. So, we have to get these busy thoughts out of our head and on to paper. They need to live somewhere else.

BADASS HOMEWORK

Get out a journal or the notes on your phone. I keep this on my phone so it goes everywhere with me. And every Sunday night, I create my week. I list every day of the week and then list all I need to get done each day. This takes some initial set up but it's totally worth it. Think about how awesome it's going to be to stop feeling so overwhelmed. Then each day, list what you need to get done and use the following formula:

A. Things you'll get done in the morning

B. Things you'll get done in the afternoon

C. Things you'll get done before the end of the day

D. Things you can delegate to someone else if not completed

YOU ARE A BADASS MOM

Then I also keep a note called "I Am a Badass Mom." Because I am, and this title just sounds better. A "To Do" list is so 2008. Whenever anything pops in my head that I need "to do," especially those things that feel overwhelming, I put them on this list. And then they're gone. I still need to take action on them, but at least they're out of my head. That frees up so much space for me to think about the things that matter most. Like how I'm going to buy my dream home and how my kids will take care of me when I'm older and take me on a luxury vacation to Italy. The really important stuff. See, freeing your mind of your "to do's" gives you time to be present and gives you time to visualize what you really *do* want. Goodbye, overwhelm. Hello, next-level life.

Anytime you have a free minute and need to focus, look at your "I'm a Badass Mom" list and knock something out. And when you make your weekly list on Sunday (or whatever day works for you), then look to that list and see how you can incorporate some of those into your week.

Outsourcing

Now, what about those things that have been on that list for a long time? Or those things that keep getting pushed from one day to the next and never get done? You need to *outsource* that shit. I know this second big O word is seriously taboo to most moms. Why is it that we think we need to do it all? That's insane. And guess what? The most successful and accomplished moms who also spend time with their kids and have a great relationship, *don't do it alone*. They have a secret weapon: a nanny, an assistant, a housekeeper, whatever it looks like—they have help! Don't buy into this one-woman-show shit. It doesn't exist.

And I know what comes next. "But I don't have enough money to hire an assistant or get any help." I'm going to throw the bullshit flag on that one too. Because *yes, you do*. You are a badass and you can create anything you want in this life. Asking for help and outsourcing is probably the missing link to your manifestation. Actually it *is* the missing link to your manifestation. Guaranteed. Once you start living as if anything's possible then anything is possible. When I bit the bullet and got an assistant, here's how she *saved* me money:

- ✓ She takes me to and from the airport at a much cheaper rate. Instead of a $50–$60 taxi, she costs under $30 per trip.

- ✓ She submitted a $600 claim to insurance for me from an ER trip in Mexico (don't ask) that I *never* would have gotten around to: $600 savings.

- ✓ She returns things that would sit in my car for months and go unreturned. Unlimited amount of money saved.

✓ She buys gifts for kids' birthday parties and teachers and soccer coaches. Relationships *saved*.

✓ She booked a character breakfast for us when we had a quick visit to Disney planned. They were almost booked and I would have never made it happen. Priceless.

This is just a short list of the miraculous ways she helps our family. I can never express what a blessing it is to have her. When we flew home from a trip recently, I asked her to get us some groceries. Waiting at home were all the groceries we needed for the week, plus an organic rotisserie chicken and all the fixings for a healthy taco dinner (so we didn't have to order a pizza...again), and a beautiful bottle of wine. Seriously. That all cost me about $22 plus the cost of the groceries. If that's not worth it, I don't know what is.

BADASS HOMEWORK

Pull out your journal and make a list of all that overwhelms you. Let's call them your energy drains.

What physical things do you do every week that drain your energy? All those things that it's hard to find time to do.

If it helps you can organize them in two lists. Energy drains and energy gains. Leave everything you don't like doing in the energy drains list and everything you do enjoy in the energy gains list.

Now let's focus on the energy drains list. And write "BADASS" next to the things that only you can do. Like organize the kids' clothes. Or pick out the right cake for your daughter's birthday. (Although I might outsource that one, too.)

And write "New BFF" next to the things you can outsource—because this new person will become your new best friend. Or maybe you already have a nanny, housekeeper, or assistant who you just need to allow to do more for you.

This list will help you prioritize what you need to be doing and all the things that your New BFF can help you with. Then transfer that list over to a new note on your phone. And this now becomes the list where you keep everything that your new assistant can help you with.

I can't wait to hear how this goes for you. When we really shift our mindset around overwhelm and apply these simple outsourcing tricks to it, we can start living a more present, Badass Mom next level life.

Here's a list to get your ideas flowing.

Get These Off Your Plate:

House & Home:
- Home organization
- House cleaning
- Laundry
- Meal prep (actually almost ALL meals, even snack prep, rocks) *Smoothies….I kid you not, I have green smoothies prepped and delivered weekly.)
- Snow removal
- Lawn care
- Planting
- Homework help, tutoring
- Packing / unpacking during a move (and for vacay)
- Schedule service calls
- Waiting for service persons/deliveries

Holidays and special occasions:
- Addressing/mailing greeting cards
- Party planning
- Arrange catering details
- Holiday decorating and removal (this is the best) Outdoor holiday

Errands:
- Post Office
- Fed Ex/UPS store
- Personal delivery
- Dry cleaning
- Gift returns/exchanges (this is the bomb)
- Pick up/ drop off prescriptions
- Drop off donations (like daily)
- Return/ pick up library materials (that reminds me…)
- Photos transferred/printed
- Electronics repair

Travel:
- Packing/unpacking
- Booking airline tickets and car rentals
- Make and confirm dining reservations

Research:
- Summer Camps
- Sports Teams and other activities
- Online comparison shopping

lights (because, seriously, your marriage might be in jeopardy if you do it yourself)

Pet care:
- Walking
- Grooming
- Annual veterinary visit

Auto care:
- Regular Maintenance
- Repairs
- Wash
- Fuel

Shopping:
- Groceries
- Gifts
- School supplies
- Craft supplies
- Pet supplies
- Birthday Gift Bags
- Teacher Gifts
- Crossing Guard Gifts
- Mailman, Garbage Man, UPS Man or Women Gifts

- Insurance rates
- What size drum kit will work in my space
- What is the best karaoke machine for our basement

Business:
- Maintaining mailing lists
- Correspondence
- Scheduling appointments/clients
- Website maintenance
- Filing
- Photocopying
- Administrative Tasks
- Bookkeeping
- Social Media

Not mentioned above:
- Sorting toys in the basement (this can literally be a weekly chore)
- Picking up kids from various activities
- Making Valentines (don judge)
- Replacing the glass on the iPad for the 3rd time
- Getting new ballet shoe that your daughter outgrew in a week

###

You get the picture. Pick one or many and get started.

The Power of Letting Go

One last thing to mention about our state before moving on: There's great power in letting go.

A few months ago I sat down to meditate and I found myself saying, "Let go!"

It replaced my mantra so I went with it. And with every exhale... I let it go.

I let go of the two pounds I felt like I gained over the weekend.

I let go of the bowls of cereal still sitting on the kitchen table.

I let go of the resentment towards a friend who never apologized.

I let go of the thought that I should have

more of my shit together.

I let go over planning.

I let go of my negative thoughts about sugar and candy.

I let go of control.

I let go of my grief.

I let go of the fact that my house isn't perfect but I want it to be.

I let go of my fears.

I let go of my limits.

I let go of the illusion that my kids should be different then they are.

I let go of the fallacy that my husband should be more positive and helpful.

I let it *all* go.

It's these thoughts that hold me down, not my circumstances. If I can let them go, then I can be free. Simple as that. There's power in the process.

This simple focus on letting go has helped me tremendously in my relationship. When I let things go, when I control my reactions, we are better to each other. We're more connected and more in love. It's the #1 thing that has helped our relationship get to the next level.

More loving. More supportive. More adoring. More romantic. All of it. Because of letting go.

Now I know what you're thinking. Why me? Why do I have to be the one to let go?

And here's why... because you're the f***ing light. You're the badass. You're the one that can handle it. Because you're built for this.

If you can grow a human in your uterus, you can certainly let shit go. Our thoughts are our job. No one else's. We can choose to hold on to them and let them slowly eat away at us or we can let them go. The choice is ours. Choose wisely.

AWAKENING 3:

Your Story

SO, WE CREATE OUR thoughts, and our thoughts create our reality, right? Then who's ready to change their thoughts? (Picture me raising my hand high.)

A thought is a unit of metal energy that can now be measured scientifically. Quantum physics says we are all energy. Everyone can take control of their lives' destiny when we take charge of our thoughts. This isn't just one of my beliefs, it's scientific fact.

Our thoughts become the tone of our lives. The Universe will begin to match that tone. We need to change our thoughts if we want to change our reality. If you're ready to skyrocket your life to another level, then you need to get rid of the old stories that no longer serve you, shift limiting beliefs, and align yourself with the next-level life that you truly deserve.

This is usually where my clients get nervous. How can I change my thoughts? They're automatic.

Automatic Negative Thoughts

The truth is that you control your thoughts— they don't control you. There's no master puppeteer up in the sky telling you what to think and what not to think. When we can get that, really get that, then game over. All the pain and suffering can disappear. I know it sounds easier said than done, and I'm here to hold your hand through this process because this is one of my favorite things to teach and favorite tools to use in my life. Really grasping the knowledge that I am not my thoughts, that my painful thoughts are just a lie, has completely shifted the trajectory of my life. I find more peace on a daily basis than I ever thought possible. I don't take things personally. I don't get triggered as often. Yes, I still yell at my kids from time to time. (Good God, I'm not Wonder Woman.) I still get mad at my husband for staying out really late smoking cigars with his buddies. (That sounds stupid even writing it.) I'm still a work in progress. But I found many ways to shift my thoughts, and I'm happy to share all these with you.

First, we have to be aware. See, it always comes back to awareness. We have to be aware of the Automatic Negative Thoughts, ANTs, that are running around in our head. Those ANTs can be vicious. They suck the life out of us. If we have a lot of ANTs, we don't stand a chance.

YOU ARE A BADASS MOM

Who is in charge? You or the ANTs?

If you want to take your life, your love, and your parenting to the next level, if you want to really live the life of your dreams, you can't keep doing what you're doing. That means you can't keep thinking what you're thinking because again, your thoughts create your reality.

What this means is that we have created everything we are experiencing up until now, and we can choose to create anything we want from here forward. That's the power of our thoughts. Our state (that's the way we prime ourselves) plus our story (that's our thoughts) plus our strategy (that's the action we take) equals our reality. State + story + strategy = the life we're living.

So if you don't like the reality that you're living in every area of your life, if you want to enhance your relationship—change your thoughts. If you want to improve your parenting—change your thoughts. If you want more financial freedom—change your thoughts. It all comes down to mindset. Aligning your thoughts and your mindset to what you want to achieve, to the ideal that you want to create— that is essential. That is the key.

And we have to remember that it's not just thoughts, it's our words too. Our thoughts, words, and feelings create. So getting all of those in line is the master discipline.

Here's a simple story that explains how our thoughts and words create. I was in my late twenties, living in Lincoln Park—a fun, hip, young area of Chicago—and working as a director of a big health club. It was really hard to find parking where I lived. It became a perpetual struggle and I feared getting towed all the time. I thought about it a *lot*. And talked about it a *lot*. Even when I was parked legally, my thoughts immediately went to "What if I get towed?" Then one morning, after I parked in a perfect spot, my car was gone. Finally, I got towed. And oh boy, did I jump on that story bandwagon. I went straight to work, furious, and told everyone who would listen about my car being towed. I shared how I was parked legally and my car got towed. I called my mom and told her. I called my sister and told her. I told strangers on the street. I told Mike the taxi driver. I told my neighbors. I talked about it like crazy. So after work, I went to the pound, got my car out and I was still reeling about it the next day.

Two days later, perfectly legally parked, my car my car got towed *again.* I was furious. I went crazy. I went right back to work and told everyone who would listen. I ran around telling everyone that my car got towed. I called the pound, talked to eighteen different people. I finally went down there and... they admitted that it was towed accidentally. That it was completely legally parked and accidentally towed. They didn't understand it and neither did I. I didn't have to pay for it. But what a crazy story. So I kept talking about it. I kept telling people, "You won't believe this—my car got towed again!" It was my story for the week.

Before the week was over, I parked my car briefly, with my hazards on, while I ran up to a park in the city to tell some kids that their coach was on his way to their practice. I looked back over my shoulder, and my car was getting towed! For the third time! In one week! Three times in seven days my car got towed. That's how powerful our word is. That's how powerful our thoughts are. This is a simple story, but it happens in all areas of our lives, all the time. The Universe never stops placing orders. Our thoughts and words are orders to the Universe, and the Universe is always delivering on the orders we place. I placed an order and the

Universe delivered. I placed another order and the Universe delivered. I should expect the order to show up.

When I place an order on Amazon, I know and trust that it will show up. So why when I place a solid, powerful order from the Universe, do I expect anything different? In this case, the Universe delivered even faster than Amazon. When we talk about it and think about it, we should always expect the order to show up. It's not airy fairy or woo woo. It's science.

Subconscious Thoughts

The Universe isn't listening to only our conscious, dominant thoughts and words. It responds to our subconscious thoughts too. When I started studying the law of attraction and quantum physics, I also dove deep into neuroscience. You have to. They're all interconnected. Neuroscience research reveals that our conscious thoughts make up only 7%

of what we're thinking. Only 7%. Wow. We need to get the other 93% on board. So when we have a long overriding fear, worry or negative thought, we place an order. When we unintentionally expect that there will be tension at that family party: Order received. When we expect our husband to be in a bad mood: Wish granted. The only way to fix it is to be more conscious about our thoughts and to get the other 93% on board. Be more proactive. Focus on and think the thoughts you *do* want, so you're not placing orders for what you don't.

The good news is the subconscious is a yes machine, meaning it responds to every seed you plant with a yes.

"I'm feeling better." Yes.

"My relationship is improving." Yes.

"My kids are actually getting along." Yes.

"I love spending time with my in-laws." Yes.

"My business is booming." Yes.

"I see less and less cellulite on my thighs every day." Yes.

The more we program our subconscious, the more it responds. You're literally reprograming your subconscious brain. And now you need to keep reprogramming those thoughts so that those orders will be fulfilled.

I have another thoughts-creating story that was totally subconscious. When I was nineteen, I read the book *A Return To Love* by Marianne Williamson, and it totally turned my life around. It was the first time I really understood forgiveness or thought about consciously creating my life. I credit that book for starting me on this path to personal growth that I've been on for almost thirty years now. When anyone asked me how I got into this work, I would credit that book and Marianne Williamson. I hosted book clubs on that book. I went to see her speak whenever I could. I read everything else she ever wrote.

Many years later, I was volunteering at a conference called "Celebrate Your Life." (Badass conference that you must check out. #lifechanging) They have amazing speakers like Neale Donald Walsh, the late Wayne Dyer, Sonia Choquette, and Marianne Williamson to name a few. As a volunteer, you never know what job you might have. So when I got my assignment, I was so excited, but not surprised: I got assigned as Marianne Williamson's speaker's assistant. When I saw that, I knew that my subconscious placed those orders.

I got to meet her at the airport in a limo. Take her back to the hotel. Check her into her hotel room. Bring her to and from her keynote. We had many long conversations, and she was as gracious and graceful as I had ever imagined. We even did some yoga together in her hotel room before she went onstage to speak. Yeah, so that happened. #wow

At one point, she saw my book in my bag—the book I'd had since 1999, that followed me from house to house from college through adulthood. She asked if she could see it. It was dog-eared and highlighted and thoroughly used. She said it was a dream come true for an author to see a book like that and asked me if she could sign it for me. Um, yes please. What a beautiful order I had placed. More of those subconscious orders, please.

You can't expect great things when you're thinking lousy thoughts. So we need to change our thoughts. As badass moms, we need to start focusing on more of the good in our lives. We need to shift our thoughts to place the orders that we do want. To start aligning with the next-level life that we know we deserve and that's within our reach. It all starts with our thoughts.

So how do we change our thoughts?

Cancel Process

The first thing I teach all of my clients to do is to create their own unique cancel process. A cancel process is something you use to cancel a negative thought and shift to a new more powerful, positive thought. You can make this cancel process your own—it's whatever works for you. When I first designed a cancel process, it was simple: "Cancel cancel cancel" is what I used. Then I shifted it to "erase erase replace." I would erase the negative thought and replace it with a powerful, positive thought. My cancel process has evolved over time, and I'm happy to say, I don't have to use it as often as I used to. Now I use it for things like worrying that the kids might get hurt. Or afraid they're not being treated right at school. "Erase erase replace" and I think about them thriving.

My friends and clients have come up with

their own very unique cancel processes. My friend Lindsey says, "Oops, do over." My friend Andy says, "Stop cancel clear, I have nothing to fear all my love is here." My client Jeanie, when her thoughts started spiraling out of control, would sit down and talk to her thoughts as if they were a little child: "Oh, that's OK, sweetie, but that's not how it goes. Here's how the story ends." She would rewrite the story. When my kids get scared and have negative thoughts, I tell them to change the channel. They know what a TV remote is, so they picture TV remotes in their hands. We point the imaginary remotes toward their heads, and we change the channel. We cancel that thought and insert a new more peaceful thought in its place. It takes some practice, but this can literally rewire your brain.

I think of these tools like a new path in the woods. We have these paths that we've already cleared. We knocked down trees and shrubs, cleared the ground of sticks and rocks so we have a nice, clear path to walk down. It's easy and comfortable. But when you realize that the easy, comfortable path doesn't take you where you want to go, eventually, you're going to get sick of it. And you're going to have to clear a new path. A cancel process, and all the other tools I'm going to share with you, will help you start to clear a new path in the woods of your brain. It will rewire your thoughts so you'll have a new path to walk down. And this new path will take your badass self to a life you *do* want. Make sure that next-level life is juicy enough that you're eager to pick up the axe and get to work.

BADASS HOMEWORK

Create your very own cancel process. What works for you? Don't just think about it. Write it down. And commit to using it. Bonus points if you share this concept with your kids and help them create a cancel process of their own.

Affirmations

Affirmations work, too. They're another tool for this new path. And here's why they work: I picture these negative thoughts as seeds in our minds that we've been watering. If you water a seed, it's going to grow. Those negative thoughts, those seeds, are now growing, even flourishing, because we were nurturing them and watering them by thinking about them. Now there are positive, powerful thought seeds that have been planted as well. We just need to start watering those positive thoughts more than we've been watering the negative thoughts, and the more powerful positive thoughts will be fed and will thrive. Affirmations help water the positive powerful seeds in our minds. A lot of people think they're just silly, but this is why they actually do work.

Here's how you can create a new powerful affirmation for yourself. Think about one of your negative thoughts. Now turn it around. Think of the exact opposite. Here's the key: The opposite, more powerful positive thought has to be as true or truer than the negative thought. It has to be true for it to work. If we try to use affirmations that aren't true for us, affirmations that feel like bullshit, they don't fly. Our subconscious mind will be like, "Yeah, right...nice try."

Here's an example: Years ago, I had a negative thought that was limiting my life. The thought was, "I'm a terrible cook." It was a powerful one. I really was a terrible cook. I was placing orders daily for the Universe to prove to me what a terrible cook I was. Everyone around me believed it too. They joined in on the order and would agree, fanning the flames of my negative thought. So when I wrapped my head around it and decided it was a limiting belief, a thought and story that no longer served me, I decided to change it. The turnaround thought for "I'm a terrible cook" is "I'm an awesome cook." But that was bullshit. There's no way I believed that. So that would get me nowhere. A turnaround that *was* true was "I enjoy making healthy meals for my family." That was true. That was even more true than my negative thought. So that became my new affirmation. My new mantra. I wrote it on my bathroom mirror. "I enjoy cooking healthy meals for my family." And I didn't stop there. I never stop with only one limiting belief. I decided to tackle a few more things that were plaguing our family lately. So then I wrote: "We have peaceful, fun and easy mornings." "John and I are getting along great and feeling really connected." "I have the right and perfect team to support my business." See, affirmations place orders too. So do intentions, thoughts, words, stories, and feelings. Why not get them all aligned with what I do want? When I take the time to turn around my thoughts, I create a new path through the forest, and the new clearing is oh-so-much better than the old one.

BADASS HOMEWORK

Get a dry erase marker and head to your bathroom mirror (or any mirror in your house). Think about one of your negative thoughts. And then turn it around. Think of the exact opposite. Then tweak it. Make sure it's as true or truer than your negative thought. When you find a thought that is positive but also true, you've got it. Water that seed by writing it on your bathroom mirror. You can also get your kids involved. Ask them to turn a stressful, negative thought around and write it down on their mirror.

At the root of many of our limiting beliefs are a few very powerful, positive affirmations that will help. Try some of these on for size: "I am enough." "I am worthy." "I am deserving of all that is good." "I am lovable exactly as I am."

Who needs more of those seeds flourishing in their mind? Get in line behind me.

Here's a list of some other things you can do to shift your thoughts.

* Create a cancel process
* Shift into gratitude
* Move into appreciation
* Focus on forgiveness
* Breathe
* Meditate
* Move your physical body
* Put on music
* Use tapping (Emotional Freedom Technique)
* Do the Byron Katie work (more on this in the next section)
* Call a friend
* Start talking about what you *do* want
* Use Future Pulls (explanation coming)
* Read books, listen to podcasts, attend

programs, retreats and conferences

* Surround yourself with awesome people

Limiting Belief Work

The most important process I use with my clients to help them change their thoughts and turn limiting beliefs into powerful positive beliefs is the work by Byron Katie. I learned how to facilitate this work in 2003, right after my husband (who was my boyfriend of eight years at the time) checked into rehab for alcoholism and drug addiction. If it wasn't for the work, I wouldn't have this life I now have with him, because I wouldn't have given him another chance. I realized it was my thoughts, not my circumstances, that were bringing me stress. He chose drugs over me. Was that true? Byron Katie eloquently walked me through a process on that thought and with her beautiful insight, she asked me this question that led to a huge breakthrough.

"Oh, honey," she said, "do you really want it to be any different? Would you ever want to get in the way of his soul's path back to God?"

Wow. What a game changer. How could I ever say yes to that? Her work, the four questions, and the turnaround helped me to lovingly accept John's experience as his soul's experience and to forgive him. He got sober. A year later, he proposed. We got married on the tenth anniversary of our first date. And we've already celebrated our eleventh wedding anniversary. I credit his sobriety first, obviously. If he didn't make this powerful choice to live a life of sobriety, we wouldn't be together. And we wouldn't have our children, these amazing souls who joined us on this journey. He wouldn't have the success he has, the health he has, the character he has, the relationships he has. None of it. But if I didn't do the work on my thoughts, I don't know if I could have forgiven him. The Work is what helped me get over myself and support him through his recovery. And because of that we've created this amazing life.

Byron Katie created a process that will change your stressful thoughts from thoughts that you feel are challenging and hurtful to something that has no power over you. She does this with four questions and a turnaround. Here are the questions.

Is this thought true?

Do you absolutely know it's true?

How do you feel, when you believe that thought?

Where would you be without that thought?

Then you turn it around to the exact opposite and try and find a thought that's more powerful and more positive but that's equally as true. Her whole premise is that it's our thoughts that cause our suffering, not our circumstances. When we believe the lie that things should be any different than they are, we will suffer. When we love what is, and accept things exactly as they are, we'll find peace. There's always peace on the other side of a stressful thought, and this process is the best way I've ever found to get there.

More on Katie's profound process and a lot of free courses can be found at www.thework.org.

The Power of Intention

The author Wayne Dyer has a whole book on the power of intention. I see so many people who pay no attention to the intention they put out there. Again we're placing an order with every intention. Big and small. When I set a conscious intention that my husband won't communicate with me, guess what happens? Yep. You got it. When I set an intention that the kids will misbehave, you betcha… whining, complaining, fighting galore. There is *power* in our intentions, so we need to be more intentional about them.

I launched a rocket of desire before this school year for the right and perfect teacher. I got specific in my request. I asked the Universe for a teacher who was positive. Focused on gratitude. Catered to all learning styles. Very sweet and nurturing. Used a lot of verbal and visual cues. A great communicator. And who really understood my daughter's needs for breaks and movement.

I can say with 100% certainty that I got the right and perfect teacher for my kids this year. And I truly believe it was through the power of intention.

I start everything with intention now. My husband and I went on a trip that he won through his work on a cruise down the Rhine river. The people attending are not my normal tribe. Luckily, I was already into this concept that our thoughts create our reality. So I set a powerful intention to meet some like-minded people. Like-minded people at a trip that starts in Amsterdam with a bunch of car guys. Show me what you got, Universe. On the second day of our trip, I met an amazing woman at lunch. For some reason (guided by the Universe, obviously), I asked her what books she was into. And oh, wow, did that open the floodgates. We had read 90% of the same books. Was she like-minded? 1000%. We spent the rest of the week together. And you can bet your ass that whenever we go on another one of these trips, I set another powerful intention. Intention is a *powerful* thing. When is the last time you got really specific about your intention for something in your life? Now might be a great time to start.

Focus on the Good

One more way we can shift our thoughts, and therefore shift our reality, is to focus on the good. In every situation, we can find a lot of good. We can also find problems, or ways something could be better, or how we would prefer something. But there's always so much good.

Last year, we went on a trip to Mexico after the holidays.

I try and enter into every vacation thinking it will be amazing and setting some powerful intentions. Lots of quality time with the kids. A beautiful romantic connection with my husband. More fun than you can ever imagine. Perfect weather. Sunny beach days. Great food. Interesting new friends. I could go on and on. This trip to Mexico was no different. We had a beautiful room at our favorite hotel, warm sunny weather. What could go wrong?

YOU ARE A BADASS MOM

Well, as you know, when you're traveling with kids, anything and everything can go wrong. The kids might whine and fight. A lot. The taxi might take *forever*. You might get booked into the wrong room and have to move. Your son could get sick and you could spend three hours in the ER on day two, only to see him suffering for the next four days with a fever that won't break. Yeah, we've all been there. Traveling always sounds more glamorous than it is. After a trip like that, we have a choice: Share the drama or focus on the good. Everyday moms would share the drama. But we're not everyday moms. We're badass moms. The first thing an everyday mom would do is tell the dramatic tale of how her son got sick and it ruined their vacation. We feel more comfortable sharing the hardships than the highlights. Well, I'm not buying into the bullshit rule that says that you have to share the drama. Or even the reality. I find a way to focus on the good, to highlight what went *well*. I'll share the triumphs, the laughter, the sweet moments we shared. All the amazing memories we created.

On this trip, in addition to all the misfortunes I just mentioned, we also had the best New Year's Eve we've ever had as a family. We stumbled upon a fun show and beach dance party. My daughter and I had a late night fun adventure on the beach, releasing a tadpole that she named Nemo and really wanted to bring home but decided to finally set free. When the kids went to sleep, we got to ring in the New Year, just the two of us, and watched some fireworks exploding over the ocean. Romance— check.

On New Year's Day, we had a late night beach fire ceremony. As a family, we wrote down things that no longer served us, that we'd like to leave behind. (Jack being sick was on all our lists.) And things we wanted to create in the new year. I loved reading their lists. What beautiful intentions these kids can set. We lit the list on fire in a homemade fire pit and then shouted our intentions into the wind and ended with a family haka ceremony. Now how can I let that get overshadowed by a few bumps in the road?

It's all about where you put your focus. Do you focus on what went wrong, the fighting, the sickness, the delays? Or what went right: the morning breakfast buffet with food we all loved, the quiet time by the pool, the Zumba water aerobics, the jogs on the beach with my love. Backflips in the pool. The kindness of strangers. Feeding the fish in the pond and counting sixteen turtles. Reading a full book cover to cover.

When you focus on what went right, on all the good, what is there to complain about? Life happens. You choose how to respond to it. You choose what you focus on.

As we got in the taxi to the airport, I asked my kids to tell me their three favorite moments of the vacation. We came up with twenty-five, at least. We can sit and reflect on the stress and the problems. And create a story of a nightmare vacation, where things went wrong and we may never go back. *Or* we can focus on all the moments of beauty and connection. The quality time that wouldn't have happened at home. The new experiences that expanded our horizons. The swimming and the dancing and falling asleep in each other's arms. That's what I'll focus on. And soon we'll forget that Jack got sick. I might remember how nice the doctors were and how taken care of we felt. It won't be a bad memory. But a good one. More of that, please.

So here's how to get a better order from the Universe and have a great experience traveling with your kids. *Focus only on the easy parts. Focus only on the peace, not the stress.* There are as many moments of those when you look for them. And the more you look for them, the more you'll create them. And you'll head into blissful amnesia before your next trip. Focus on the good.

Happiness

Now you're ready to get happy! Now you're aware of who you are and what's going on inside you. Your state is in the right place, you're primed and ready for your day, for your week, for your month, and to have an amazing badass year. Your thoughts are tuned in to what you ideally want. You know how to handle your triggers and you know how to control those ANTs that are running around. How to turn around a thought and create a powerful positive new one. How to use your new tools to create a new path in the forest of your mind.

Now, finally, you can get happy.

Here's the thing—your happiness is the art of allowing it all in. The way that we allow in this next-level life, a life we really love, is through our happiness. Think about your happiness as a way to tune you into that dial on the radio that will let you receive the station with all that you're wanting. Your happiness will get you there. I went to an Abraham Hicks workshop many years ago called "The Art of Allowing." I had a few big dreams that I hadn't manifested yet, and I was so excited to hear, straight from the source, exactly what I needed to do. Did I need to add some crystals into my bedroom? Do I need to sleep on a bed of magnets? Do I need to tap my head and rub my belly? What is it? I didn't care—I just wanted to know why was I not allowing these things in? I was clear on what I wanted. I'd changed my thoughts. My state was in the right place. I was ready. I arrived at the workshop, open, willing and excited to hear the secret. And here's what it was all about... just how happy can you be. Just how happy can you be? It was so beautifully simple. It blew me away. Our joy and happiness can be simple, but not always easy. How can we be happy about our relationship if it's not where we want it to be? How can we be happy with our kids if they are misbehaving? How can we be happy with our career or our financial life if they're not meeting the mark?

Here's the good news: You don't need to be happy about that exact thing in order to shift and allow in what you do want. You just need to focus more on what you do want and less on what you don't want, and get happy about whatever you can get happy about. You can get happy about holiday cups at Starbucks. You can get happy about a homemade blueberry muffin. (I once cried over a really good blueberry muffin. Literally.) You can get happy petting your puppy. Anything that makes you happy will help tune you in to that radio station, to that frequency that you want to be on. That frequency that has all your desires and that's tuned in to your next-level life.

This lesson is all about flow. It's about letting go. It's about following your heart guidance and not letting your head chatter get in the way. It's about releasing the oars so your boat can turn and start floating downstream. I picture it like this: We're struggling to do do do all day. We have so much on our plates. As busy moms with careers, with relationships, we're hustling hustling hustling. And all we're doing is picking up some oars and paddling upstream against the current—while everything we want is downstream. All we need to do is let go of the oars. The boat will turn itself—it will turn downstream and start floating with the current. So just toss them into the water. Actually, don't litter—donate them to a local charity. But stop paddling with them. Your boat will float downstream gracefully and easily towards everything that you are wanting if you just stop paddling so hard upstream. And start focusing more on your daily happiness.

We need to safeguard our happiness like it's our *job*, like our life depends on it. Because it does. See, no one else is responsible for our happiness. We are. No one's coming to our rescue and making sure we have a cushy, easy, happy day every day. That's our job. But we can't do that if we don't know what makes us happy. What lights you up inside? What helps your boat float downstream?

BADASS HOMEWORK

Make your happy list. When I first did an exercise like this many years ago, I called it my "in the zone" list. When my life was really in the flow, what was I doing that made me feel good? What made it a great day? And some of the things on that list were: exercising, getting outside in nature, eating healthy, meditating, spending time with John, laughing with friends.

I've tweaked it over the years. I'm always adding to what I now call My Happy List. I teach this to all my clients, and everyone's list is unique.

It's a fun thing to do and share with other badass moms, because they'll come up with some ideas that you never thought of, and you'll add to theirs as well. One of my clients said it made her really happy to wear red lipstick. So I asked her how often she wore it. About once a month was her answer. Well, if you're going through a rough patch in your life and red lipstick makes you happy, you need to wear red lipstick every damn day. You need to put that red lipstick on first thing when you get out of bed in the morning. And she did.

Sometimes, it can be that simple. An easy

shift and a way to really apply something that makes you happy.

What are those things that you can do every day, little and big, that make you happy? Drink that green tea you love. Eat some dark chocolate. Have a nice glass of red wine. Light some candles. Having my house in order and organized is on my new happy list. Wearing clothes that make me feel great is on my new happy list. You'll notice that when a day did not go great, it's because you didn't do anything on that list. When a day is awesome, it's probably because you knocked off a bunch of things on that list.

And here's another great thing: When your day is not going well and you're aware of it (hint, hint: awareness is the master discipline), you can turn your day around by focusing on your happy list.

One day recently, my daughter, Zoe, and I

were at Target, rushing through the store, grabbing some groceries and some household items we needed. I had had a really busy day, and my after-school sitter had canceled. So I picked Zoe up from kindergarten and took her with me to run errands. I missed my workout.

Neither of us had eaten and we were having a miserable time. She was snatching things off the shelf and throwing little tantrums, and I was fed up. I wasn't tolerating any of it. I was about to send my husband a nasty text, telling him how miserable I was. You know those sniper bullets we send to our spouse, even though we know they can do nothing about it.

Luckily, I got present and had an awakening. I realized this was my responsibility—100% my responsibility. And I took my happiness back.

I picked Zoe up, left that half-full cart sitting in the middle of the aisle in Target. We walked out of that store, had some food, and had a great time together. I spent quality time with her. I was out in the sunshine. Ate something I loved (probably a blueberry muffin). I listened to some great music, and soon, I had done five or six things on my happy list and was feeling amazing again.

You have to understand: there are things on my happy list that aren't on anyone else's. For instance, I love to coach people. I love to listen to their challenges and their struggles and help them feel lighter. That might drain someone else.

A few years ago, when we were moving from our home in the city to our dream home in the suburbs, I spent the morning at IKEA with a friend. Shopping at IKEA is on her happy list, but it's not on mine. It's on my hell list. I then came home and continued to pack for our move. That's not on my happy list either.

STEFFANI LEFEVOUR

As my husband was on his way home, I realized I was empty. I was drained. My battery was depleted, and I was ready for him to walk in the room with the kids and snap all their heads off. But again, I realized I'm responsible for my happiness. No one else is.

So I dropped it all. Everything I was doing. I went outside, jumped on my Vespa scooter, and drove down to the beach. Went for a quick run while listening to some awesome music and was back home in thirty minutes to greet them with open arms and a smile on my face. I knocked off about eight things on my happy list: being outside exercising, being in the sunshine, being on the beach, listening to music. I grabbed a green tea on my way home. I got to ride my Vespa. I had some free time and freedom for myself. All of those things are on my happy list. So I was fully charged again.

Our happiness is important. We need to

safeguard our happiness like our life depends on it. When safeguarding your happiness becomes a natural thing, and when we teach our kids that they are responsible for their happiness, no outside circumstances and no other people, then we can live our lives in flow. We can live our lives in the zone, and we will want for nothing more.

Future Pulls

Here's one of my favorite processes to change your thoughts and step into a life you're really excited about. It's called a future pull. And it's a beautiful way to get into that *feeling* place that is the most powerful place to create from. Here's how it works: You simply talk about something as if it's already happened. It's even more powerful if you get your friends involved. When I taught law of attraction workshops out of my house, many years ago, before it was a common thing (yes, I was that girl), I would put people into groups of three, and one person would get to go first. The other two people would then talk about the first person's big desire as if it already happened. And the person whose dream was being manifested would just sit there with their eyes closed and *feel* it. It feels amazing. Step into that vision. Really feel what it's like to create what you want. And it's on its way to you.

One summer, we rented a house in New Buffalo, Michigan. A dream home on the beach with a pool and amazing views of the sunset. It was such a beautiful home—I was crazy about it. While living there, I felt like it was ours. I talked about it like it was ours. We wanted to buy a summer home on the lake so I future-pulled the crap out of it. I would stand on the deck looking over the water, thinking, "I'm so happy and grateful this house is mine." It wasn't even for sale, but I could see it as ours. I asked the rental agency if they would ask the owner if they'd be willing to sell it. Her response was, "You're not the first person to ask. I'm sure he's not in the market to sell right now." But I kept dreaming about that house. And one month later, the agency called me and said he'd consider selling it to us. And I'm happy to say, we bought that house. Future pulls work. They align you with your desire even faster than you can imagine. When you get into that feeling place of that dream come true, nothing can stand in the way of you receiving it.

Here's one more quick future pull story. When I was twenty I worked at an Italian restaurant in my hometown as a hostess. Hung on the wall next to my hostess stand were photos of famous people like Frank Sinatra and Sammy Davis Jr. At that time I wanted to be a famous singer. So I would tell everyone working there that I would be on that wall someday. We would all joke about it. I would play with different stage names and talk about how great

I looked in the photo. I was young just playing around with this interesting concept called the law of attraction. And then one day, there was a local newspaper that came in and shot some photos and wrote a story on the restaurant. That paper was published and this young hostess was in the photo. Guess where they hung that photo? Right on the wall next to Frank and Sammy. This. Shit. Works. It worked then, and it works now.

BADASS HOMEWORK

I hope you have someone in your life you can do a future pull with. Someone who believes in this airy fairy woo woo stuff like you do. Yeah, that someone. Call them up now and do a future pull. You can text it to someone, too.

"Hey, you know that raise I've been dying to get, well I just got it and it was *way* bigger than I had even hoped for."

YOU ARE A BADASS MOM

Talk about that thing that you want to create as if it's already happened. It can be the weight you've lost and how effortless it was. It can be your new and improved relationship with your insanely romantic husband. It can be your kids thriving at school with impeccable behavior. Whatever your focus is lately, that area that you'd most like to improve.

Do a future pull on it. It will help you get into the *feeling* place of that dream coming true and that will help it manifest even faster.

AWAKENING 4:

Your Vision

CAN YOU IMAGINE a life where you are aware of your thoughts? You're stepping fully into your higher self. You know how to handle your triggers, you've shifted you're limiting beliefs, you've been focusing on your state and have yourself primed every day to handle any challenges that are coming your way. Your stories align with what you do want. Your thoughts create a reality that you love and that you're excited about. And you focus on your happiness every day doing things that bring you so much joy fulfillment and contentment.

That's what these awakenings can do for you.

Now how can we maintain all that? It's easy to read about these strategies in a book but it's a lot harder to apply them all.

Here's what's worked for me.

Boundaries

Many badass moms don't have clear boundaries. We're obligers by nature. We want to keep the peace. And make sure everyone is happy. Boundaries have less to do with how people treat us and more to do with what we say "no" to. We need to set some boundaries around those six pillars and around our time and relationships. When we set clear boundaries, everyone wins.

My coach asked me, a few years ago, if I was an obliger. "What do you mean?" I asked. And before she could answer, all of my "obliging" came flooding back to me. Like a movie reel. I could see time and time again how I went out of my way to "oblige" other people. Never putting myself first. It's been a long, obliging road. We say yes to school commitments, yes to hosting, yes to lead the kids' games at the block party, yes to picking up our friend from the airport. (Wait—that's what your new BFF is for.) We sacrifice our state and our happiness when we set weak boundaries.

God forbid we hurt someone's feelings or let someone else take on the responsibility. I've obliged my way through partnerships that no longer served me. Through jobs that I should have left years ago. In relationships that had run their course. In friendships that were clearly meant for a season not a lifetime. Even obliging others who I've lent big amounts of money but I don't want to ask them about it for fear that it might hurt their feelings.

(Seriously?) I'm an obliger. Clearly.

And what that means to me now is that I need more boundaries. I need more self love. I need to put myself first and need to oblige *me*. When I can do that, I can consciously create a life I *do* want. Not one that's dictated by other people's agendas.

It's an uphill climb. But with awareness, my obliging others habit doesn't stand a chance. Start by creating more boundaries.

BADASS HOMEWORK

Listen, you know what you need to say "no" to. And you know where you need to create more clear boundaries. But you're just not doing it. So get out your note pad or journal and start writing it down.

What do I need to say "no" to?

What duties or tasks can I *allow* someone else to take on?

Where do I need to create more clear boundaries?

Who do I need to create more clear boundaries with?

What do I have to *do* in order to set these boundaries?

Many times when we have a little process like this we overthink it and feel like we won't have any clear answers. When that happens to me, I still put pen to paper and see what comes out. It's often surprising how much I do know when I don't let my head talk me out of it. It also helps to ask this question.

What does my soul think I need to say "no" to?

Who does my soul think I need more clear boundaries with?

Apply that soul-level thinking to all of those questions if you're feeling stumped, and I promise you'll come up with some really beautiful answers.

Surround Yourself With Great People

One important factor in maintaining this next-level life you're creating is who you surround yourself with. Author and motivational speaker Jim Rohn said, "You are the average of the five people you spend the most time with." And when we really look at that, we realize how true it is. If you want to take your relationship the next level, how are the relationships of the people you're closest with? If you want to raise the bar in your health and fitness, surround yourself with people who are the healthiest and fittest people you know. If you want to improve your parenting, are you hanging out with moms who really raise you up and raise the bar? Or are you adding to the drama and complaints on the soccer field?

STEFFANI LEFEVOUR

Years ago, I read the Harvard Grant Study. It's a study that spanned more than seventy-five years studying the physical and emotional habits and experiences of 268 Harvard college men. It basically explained that the connections you have with the people closest to you will not only determine how happy you are, but will also determine your level of wealth and success, the longevity and quality of your marriage, your level of health and wellness, and how happy and fulfilled you live your life. That's pretty much everything. And it all comes down to the quality of your relationships.

That hit me hard. I looked around at my closest relationships and realized that 90% of them were not chosen—they were convenient. They consisted of co-workers, neighbors, teammates, gym friends, family members. And they were fine, even somewhat fulfilling, but were they taking me everywhere I wanted to go in life? Bottom line was no. Could they be better? Hell, yes. So I set out to find my tribe and see how that might enhance my life. It didn't take long to find them, and *wow* was it a game changer. I am now determined to create more tribes for badass moms who, like me, refuse to settle.

You need to find a tribe. Find a tribe of the right women who are also interested in their next-level life. Who are interested in living as their highest selves. Who know and accept their Universal assignments. Who know who they need to be in order to step into that highest version of themselves. That can be a neighbor, a best friend, your local community of moms. They can be in your backyard or online. But it's been proven that a tribe can help take us farther than we can go alone. This tribe or community is crucial. And the quality of the women in your tribe is crucial, too.

BADASS HOMEWORK

Warning: this is not going to be easy. And it's usually a harsh reality check for most of us. Before you do this homework, take a deep breath, and remember that no one will ever see this sheet of paper. Remind yourself what an honest, fair, non-judgmental and loving person you are. And then, write down the names of all the people you spend the most time with. Some might be family members, some might be your kids' friends' moms, some might be co-workers. Who do you spend the *most* time with? Now look closely at that list. Is there anyone on that list that you want to spend less time with? If so, mark a minus next to their name. If you're fine with the amount of time you spend with that person and you don't want to spend more or less, write an equal sign next to their name. If you want to spend more time with someone, write a plus sign next to their name. Now, make a plan to spend more time with those plus people. And a plan to let the minus people fall off. I know it sounds harsh but sometimes just bringing awareness to it can help make it happen fairly effortlessly. One more thing to write down: Are there people in your life who aren't on that list but who you'd love to spend more time with? Write them down, put a plus next to their name, and make a plan.

If you're still looking for your tribe, you know I've got one for you. Join my Badass Mom Society Facebook group that I've mentioned earlier in this book. You might even find some new local friends in this tribe.

www.facebook.com/groups/badassmomsociety/

Upper Limit Problems

There's one more big factor involved in creating and maintaining your new next level life, and that's to be aware of your upper limits. There's a beautiful book called *The Big Leap* by Gay

Hendricks that explains upper limit problems very eloquently. In essence, an upper limit problem is a mindset, an invisible upper limit that we have in place. It's a way in which we put a lid on our life and our potential. And when we're not aware of it, it can really keep us down. I've seen it in my life and with many of my clients. The minute we try and crank up one area of our lives, another area of our life takes a turn for the worse. That's an undercover upper limit problem.

Think about it like you have your thermostat set at 80 degrees, and you realize through your awareness that you want to turn up the heat in your health and fitness. So you start a new workout regimen, you add green smoothies into your diet, you find friends who become workout partners and meet you at the gym, you start taking the supplements that have been sitting in your cabinet forever. You turn that dial up to 85. But you're not ready for that temperature. And then things start getting worse in your love relationship. You're fighting with your husband or you're not making time for each other. Communication is not where it needs to be. You're both getting resentful and bitter. See, the thermostat is used to being set at 80 degrees so when you turned it up to 85, it turned another area down to 75 so that you would be set back at 80 overall. It usually happens in the areas of health and fitness, love relationship, financial life, or parenting.

My husband and I noticed an upper limit problem a few years ago. He was working out more, eating healthy, getting in the best shape of his adult life. His business was booming and we had more financial freedom than we ever thought possible. And we were fighting. A lot. He would come home from work ready for a fight and things were just spiraling out of control. Luckily, I had stumbled on the book *The Big Leap* at that exact time. Thank you,

Universe. We sat down and talked about our upper limit problems. I explained to him what it was and I asked him directly if he thought this might be an upper limit issue. He said "Hell, yes." It's like we just internally can't handle all this goodness that's coming our way. We're not ready for our lives to be great in every area. Until we're *aware* of it, we can't adjust. So we need to be aware of our upper limits. We need to *consciously* turn the heat up and be prepared to live our lives set to that new level. Just being aware of the upper limit issues can be the key. Adding in some affirmations that we are ready to live in abundance, that we're ready to take our life to the next level, can really help too.

Plan Your Next Adventure

The next thing we all need to step into this bigger, better life is to have the next big thing planned. This book will turn into a "shelf help" book if you don't continue to take action toward your next-level life and do the work it takes to really be your highest self. So plan the next book you're going to read. Plan the next course you're going to take. Sign up for that retreat. Finally join that mastermind group. Having the next thing planned keeps you plugged in and energized to continue this momentum to keep taking your life to the next level.

You can and will maintain all of this momentum if you're aware of your upper limits. You plan the next big thing and you find your tribe and surround yourself with other people who are doing this work. The best way that I have continued to shift my upper limits and take my life to the next level is accountability. Having other women hold you accountable is key. If you want to join me on another adventure, I always have fun things planned. Send me an email at info@myhappilife.com and I'll reply back with everything on the badass calendar.

Accountability

The only difference between where you are and where you want to be is what you do. The action you take and the daily habits you create are holding you back or moving you forward. Accountability is the key to creating new daily habits. We often do more for others than we will do for ourselves.

I've been hosting masterminds and accountability groups for more than twenty years. I started my first group right out of college. It was an actors' group. I was a theater major in college and started pursuing an acting career when I moved to the city. One of my acting teachers told me that I had to surround myself with other actors. So I started a group. We met monthly and set some goals. Because of that group, I kept submitting my headshots to my dream agent. Because of that group, I signed with that dream agent. Because of that group, I kept honing my skills and landed some great work. That group was the catalyst to many, *many* groups to come. I have now run accountability/mastermind groups for *everything* in my life. I've run health and fitness groups, parenting groups, law of attraction groups. I started an accountability group with twelve of my favorite entrepreneurs who helped me start my business. I've had accountability for my love relationship, for de-cluttering my house, for upgrading my life. Literally everything. Having someone or a group hold you accountable can take your life to a totally new level.

Say yes

Another way to maintain this next-level badass mom life is to say yes. And create more abundance in your life. An object in motion will stay in motion. You need to say yes to keep the ball rolling.

"But you just told us to set more boundaries and say no more often. What should we say yes to?" I look at it like this: Say yes to heart guidance. Not head chatter. Say yes to downstream action that feels good. And no to things that feel upstream and icky. Say yes to things that light you up inside and no to things that don't. Say yes to things that energize you and no to things that drain you.

You can't expect to have a first-class lifestyle without booking a first-class ticket. I mentioned this to a client years ago when I first started coaching, and then it hit me that I had never flown first class. The next day (great timing, big U), I received an email to check in to my flight down to Austin, Texas. When I clicked the link, it asked me, "Would you like to upgrade to first class?" An interesting predicament. I *just* coached someone on shifting their first-class mindset and how to follow their downstream heart guidance, and here I was with an opportunity to shift it myself. I've been doing this work long enough to know when there's a sign, I need to listen to it. So I clicked on the link and I booked the first-class ticket.

On my flight, I wrote two blog posts, designed a workshop, had a lovely breakfast, and met an amazing woman. It was definitely meant to be, but most importantly, I reveled in the fact that I was living a first-class lifestyle. I sat in that big comfortable seat, looked out the window, and celebrated my life, and all the abundance that surrounds me.

When you book a first-class ticket, that says you're not afraid. When you book a first-class ticket, you're challenging yourself to maintain a first-class lifestyle. You're placing an order to the Universe for more first-class lifestyle experiences. When you book a first-class ticket, you shout to the world, *I am worthy* and *there is enough.*

I now see sitting in first class very differently. I used to look at the people sitting in first class as I passed them by, and I would either judge them or admire them. Now I think they're brave. I think they had the courage to go there. They seized the day, they said yes. The next time you have an opportunity to fly first class, *take it*. Listen to your heart and honor your worth. If you feel drawn to do it, then say yes. Sit by the window if you can, look out over this beautiful world of ours, put your hand on your heart and whisper, "I am worthy." You'll be amazed how many more first-class experiences show up in your life. And you might even get a warm chocolate chip cookie. What is the equivalent of a first-class ticket in your life? Say yes to that.

The Climb

I know this work can be hard. As busy, working badass moms we have a shit ton on our plate.

YOU ARE A BADASS MOM

It's not easy to add to that plate. I get it. It's like a slow but steady climb up a mountain. A relationship mountain, a parenting mountain, a health mountain. All these mountains. How will we ever make it to the top. I felt that climb the most when my son was born I was thirty-eight years old and surprisingly nowhere near prepared for motherhood. He was born seven weeks early and was very colicky. He cried for the first six months of his life. I didn't know what a colicky baby was until I had one. And even then I didn't know what was happening. I think as new moms we go into survival mode, and we think that every new mom is experiencing the same thing. It wasn't until his peak of fussiness, on Halloween when he was only eight weeks old, that I realized this wasn't the norm. I had an outfit picked out for him. We planned on going trick-or-treating around the neighborhood with some other new mommies. He was crying too hard and was so uncomfortable that he popped a blood vessel in his eye. And had an umbilical hernia. As a mom, I felt like I was failing. Why is this happening to him? What am I doing wrong? Why can't I help him? If you've ever had a colicky child or spent time with one, you know the stress it creates. I don't know anything in life to compare it with. The screams of a fussy, colicky child can go right through your heart and into your soul.

I spent all day and all night in the bathroom that Halloween with the fan running and the water running and him in my arms. I had to turn out the lights and lock the doors because trick-or-treaters kept coming and I didn't want them worried. I stood there, in that bathroom, swooshing him back and forth trying to soothe him. For five solid hours. Until my arms felt like they were going to break. He would stop crying for only seconds, maybe minutes, but the second I stopped moving he would start crying again. It was torture. At my weakest moment, after hour five I broke. He started screaming again and I walked into my bedroom and dropped him down on our bed and *screamed* in his little face. "*Stop crying!*" His eight-week-old eyes looked up at me all wet with tears. At that moment I could see his fear. And I realized that I was my own worst nightmare. How could I do that to an eight-week-old? It was then I realized I was standing at the bottom of Mount Everest. And I had to start climbing.

So, that's exactly what I did, and what I *do*. Every single day.

I climb for my kids.

So they don't have a mom who acts all happy on Facebook but yells at them every night.

I climb for my husband.

So he's not married to a woman who gets resentful when he works late and punishes him by withholding sex.

I climb for my siblings.

Because they already lost one sibling and don't deserve to lose another—to anger, sorrow, frustration, or stress.

I climb for other moms.

Moms who know deep down that they deserve more and desperately want to go to the edge but are afraid to even venture out of their tents.

The journey back to happiness and up to fulfillment isn't easy. It's long, hard and treacherous at times. But one thing I know for sure is that we can't climb alone. We need a team. We need a whole village of sisters to help us up this mountain.

We need Oprah and Deepak and wine. (So. Much. Wine.)

Together, we can uncover what true happiness looks like. Hell, we can even design our own path to get there. We don't need a map. We need a *sisterhood*. We need some *accountability*. We need the right tools, support, and some dark chocolate. Then we can master this mountain together, with the right mindset and the right women. That's the tribe I'm building, with every blog, group, book and program I create

So, I'm asking you to climb. To climb *for you*, to climb *with me*, to climb for your kids, for your relationship, for the happiness that you know you deserve.

Who's with me?

Next Level

I never dreamed I'd be an author. I also never dreamed I'd be a mother. The fact that I've written a book called *You Are A Badass Mom* is practically unfathomable. This means that *anything* really is possible. And it's not just possible for me, it's possible for you too. Anything. When we put energy attention and focus into something we will create it. Like having a child. We once thought it was impossible. Then we did it. Now it's possible.

What do you want to conceive of next? Is it a better relationship? One that's romantic, loving, mutually supportive and really badass? Is it the health and fitness of your dreams? To walk down the middle of your street in a skimpy bikini, because you just love your body that much? Is it a self-care routine that really works? That lifts you up and supports your dreams and desires? Or is it being the mom you have always known is inside you? The mom who your kids need and deserve. The mom who was born the minute your first child was born but she got stuffed away with the first set of bullshit rules that everyone started feeding her. The mom who knows how to play to her own strengths and march to her own drum. The mom who is happy for no reason a lot. And knows how to let shit go.

What's your dream? A new career? Financial freedom? A kid who actually picks up after himself? I'm here to tell you it's all possible. There is nothing, *nothing* a badass mom like you can't do. When I gave birth to two babies, when I actually pushed two kids out of you know where, I knew that I was here for something bigger than myself. When I survived six months of colic, I knew I was meant for greatness. And guess what? We *all* are. No, this is not rocket science we're up to—it's bigger than that. We're here raising the next generation. Pretty important stuff.

As you move into your next level life I want you to know that I believe in you. I believe in your strength, in your ability, in your badassery. I don't just believe in it, I *know* it's all possible. When you apply all these awakenings, your higher self will take over and steer your boat toward things you've never even dreamed of before. This happened in my life and it can and will happen in yours. Do this for you and for everyone whose life you touch. When you believe in you, when you believe in what's possible, when you take downstream action towards a better life, you give everyone around you permission to do the same. You were born for this. You've got this. You are a badass mom.

Reading & Resources Mentioned

The 5 Love Languages: The Secret to Love that Lasts. Gary Chapman. 2015. www.5lovelanguages.com

The Five-Minute Journal: A Happier You in 5 Minutes a Day. Intelligent Change. 2013. Also available as an iOS or Android app

Loving What Is: Four Questions That Can Change Your Life. Byron Katie and Stephen Mitchell. www.thework.org.

The Big Leap: Conquer Your Hidden Fear and Take Life to the Next Level. Gay Hendricks. 2010.

Celebrate Your Life Conference: www.celebrateyourlife.org

Lifebook: http://mylifebook.com/

Gratitude

IN ADDITION TO the dedication at the front of this book, I have *MANY* people to thank who helped me get where I am today.

This book wouldn't be here if I didn't attend AJ Mirhzad's best-selling author book retreat. I'm SO grateful I know you, AJ. So inspired by your life and your work. And so grateful I saw your post and said yes. This has been more fulfilling than I ever thought possible.

When I signed up for the book retreat, I was planning to write another book that would have been way easier. Thank you Jessica Yarborough for believing in me and pushing me to write the book my soul longed to write. Your guidance and influence has meant the world to me. You're helping me to really live my highest truth. Nothing is more important than that.

Rhonda Britten, when you sat next to me on that bus, I had no idea what an inspiration you'd be in my life. You're the bravest, most inspiring, most fearless woman I know. Thank you for writing the foreword to this book. It means more to me than you know.

On my road of personal growth, I've been so lucky to have met so many life-changing, incredible people along the way.

To my favorite friends and accountability group, SAMETHA: we sat at a table in Mexico and declared our desires. One year later, I launched my coaching business thanks to all of you. You believed in me when I didn't, and you held me accountable. I am SO grateful.

STEFFANI LEFEVOUR

To Vishen Lakshiani and my Afest tribe: I finally found a place where I really belong. I'm truly my highest self when I'm with all of you. Thank you for pushing me to constantly to reinvent myself and for showing me what's all possible.

Jon and Missy Butcher, Sandra Garest and Lifebook: I would never have raised the bar this much in my life if I didn't have you and this Lifebook family. Lifebook blew the lid off everything I thought was possible, and you all personally showed me another level of living that I never knew existed. I'm living my dream life thanks to you.

Celebrate Your Life and Liz Dawn Donahue: A flier for CYL literally blew across my path at a gas station back in 2002. It was the sign that I was looking for. I'm so grateful I found you. You and CYL lit my fire and helped me see a life that

I never knew was possible. I can't express how much it's changed my life.

Byron Katie, your work has transformed many dark nights and turned them into bright days. I'm so grateful for The Work and all it's done for my life and the life of so many.

Katie Mark and Kelly Clement, for being my "truth" friends and holding me accountable to my highest self. For reminding me of my wings every time I forget they're there. You are the best friends I've ever had. I'm so grateful for you.

To Sandy Daulton, my parenting mentor, advisor and a great friend: your encouragement and faith in me will never be forgotten. I felt your spirit with me in every word of this book. Thanks for always showing me what really living a life filled with joy and gratitude looks like. I miss you.

To my siblings, Tam Bam, Ter Ber, and Duffer, who probably can't believe I actually wrote a book but who secretly believe I can do *ANYTHING*. I love you more than you know and more than I'll ever admit.

To Jen Cashin McDonnell, who was a friend when I really needed a friend, and who's still always there for me. "Is it HOT in here?"

ABOUT STEFFANI

STEFFANI LEFEVOUR WANTS to live in a world surrounded by ambitious, driven women who take their power back, step into their greatness, and never say no to a dirty martini.

STEFFANI LEFEVOUR

Through her passion, she's helped hundreds of women shift their mindset, transform their relationships, and live more extraordinary lives than they ever dreamed possible.

As a happiness and success coach, she's studied human potential and has been in the business of self-improvement for more than 25 years. After becoming a mom to Jack and Zoe, she had a major life shift: she realized she needed to massively transform what happiness and fulfillment looked like through this new lens of being a parent and created a new custom designed road map to success.

This new journey has led her to work on projects with many transformational leaders like Oprah Winfrey, Dr. Shefali Tsabury, and Neale Donald Walsh, all while never missing one of her son's hockey games.

When she's not chasing after her two kids, you can find her coaching, traveling, eating dark chocolate, and working by the pool at Soho House in Chicago. What lights her up most lately is running high-end Next Level Life Mastermind groups for women worldwide and posting real raw mom moments in her Badass Mom Society Facebook group.

Made in the USA
Columbia, SC
13 April 2018